The Complete
Book of the

Rugby
World Cup
1995

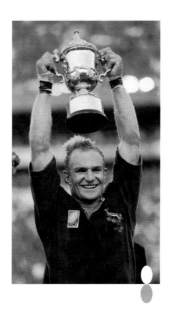

The Complete Book of the

Rugby
World Cup
1995

Edited by Ian Robertson

with Mick Cleary and Steve Bale

Photographs by
Colin Elsey and Stuart Macfarlane
(Colorsport)

Hodder & Stoughton

in association with

Scottish Life

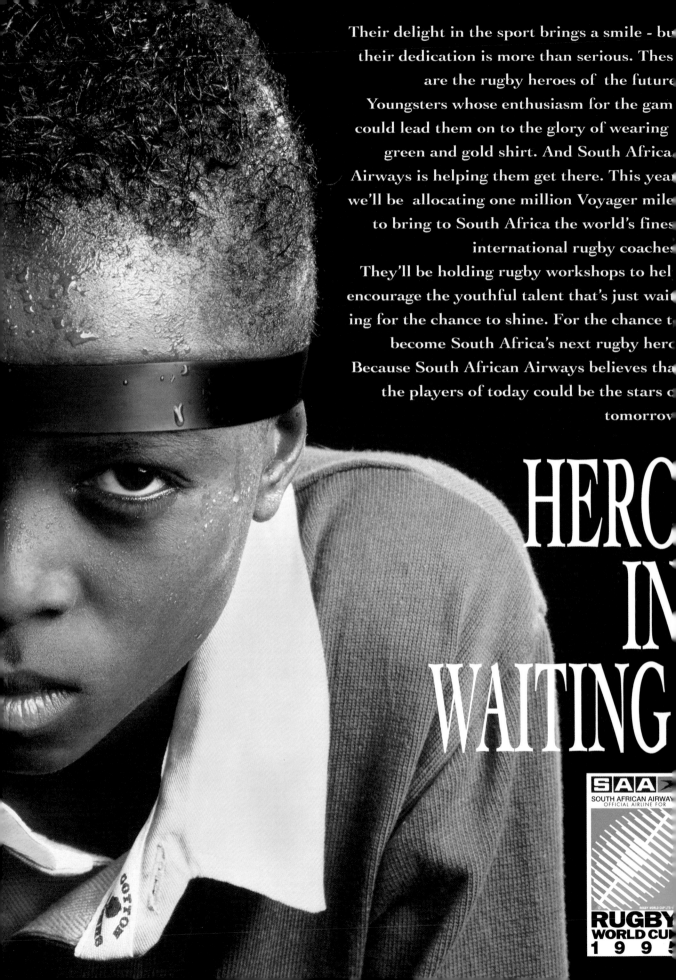

Contents

First published in Great Britain in 1995 by
Hodder and Stoughton
A division of Hodder Headline PLC

10 9 8 7 6 5 4 3 2 1

ISBN 0 340 64953 4

A CIP Catalogue record is available
for this title from the British Library

Produced by Lennard Books
A division of Lennard Associates Limited
Mackerye End, Harpenden, Herts AL5 5DR

Editor (for Lennard Books): Caroline North
Production Editor: Chris Hawkes
· Design: Design 2 Print
Cover design: Paul Cooper Design
Reproduction: Leaside Graphics

Printed and bound in Great Britain by
Butler & Tanner Ltd, Frome and London

Hodder and Stoughton
A Division of Hodder Headline PLC
338 Euston Road
London NW1 3BH

Foreword

Malcolm Murray, (extreme left) with Barry John, Bill McLaren and Ian Robertson at Ellis Park before the World Cup final.

The 1995 Rugby World Cup was a remarkable tournament which promised so much at the outset for the Grand Slam champions, England, but which ended in an all-southern hemisphere final.

The month-long festival of rugby began with a magnificent opening ceremony and each of the Home Unions had their moments of glory in the ensuing weeks. England hit the highest spot when Rob Andrew dropped the winning goal in injury time to defeat the 1991 world champions, Australia. Scotland came tantalisingly close to topping their pool, only to watch Emile Ntamack score the winning try for France in injury time. The Scots at least had the satisfaction of scoring 30 points, including three tries, against the All Blacks in the quarter-final, to become only the second side in history to get 30 points against New Zealand in an international. Ireland had two highlights: they beat Wales and scored three tries against New Zealand. Wales did almost as well as the other three Home Unions in defeat against the All Blacks.

There were some great performances from the unseeded sides, with Italy and Argentina making their mark in Pool B, and Japan delighting everyone with their courage and bravado in running in two tries against New Zealand, despite losing by a record margin.

The global audience of countless millions witnessed several brilliant individual performances,

Jonah Lomu dominating the headlines just as David Campese did in 1991. He was undoubtedly the most talked-about player of this World Cup.

But even Lomu was overshadowed by President Nelson Mandela, who set the right tone in his opening address in Cape Town and captured the hearts of the whole world at the final in Johannesburg, when he appeared on the pitch to meet the two teams wearing a François Pienaar Springbok No. 6 jersey. And, of course, what a wonderful moment it was when the President handed over the Webb Ellis Trophy to Pienaar, both leaders wearing the same jerseys.

It was impossible to top President Mandela's initiative at Ellis Park, but Pienaar came close when he replied to a question about the great support of the 60,000 fans at the final by saying, 'Don't forget the other 43 million cheering for us right round South Africa.'

The World Cup was arguably the greatest sporting event in 1995 and the memories and highlights will live on for a long time to come. This book is a fitting testament to an unforgettable tournament, and Scottish Life is very proud to be so closely associated with it.

Malcolm Murray
Chief General Manager
The Scottish Life Assurance Company

Introduction

Nic Labuschagne and Leo Williams

Nic Labuschagne.

For me as a South African the opening event was almost as significant as man stepping on to the moon. It has opened a new chapter in the history of South African rugby, and of South Africa itself. It has elevated rugby football from being the symbol of apartheid, to being the symbol of unity. It has evoked sheer pride in the sporting achievement, sheer pleasure in the way it was achieved, and sheer joy in the political implications for our – until 24 June 1995 – divided nation. The effects of this event have yet to be assessed. As a rugby man this was the highlight of my career. I said before the tournament that if South Africa reached the final, they would win it; their pride and will to win would carry them forward. I knew that they would be hungrier for victory, as it was so important for them and the country.

South Africa made tremendous improvements in self-discipline and dedication as the tournament wore on. Their control of the ball – one of their failings during the previous two to three years – has improved beyond recognition. A few superb players, like Joost van der Westhuizen, Mark Andrews, Ruben Kruger and André

Joubert; the excellent, extremely competent coach, Kitch Christie; an inspirational captain, François Pienaar, and a superb manager, Morné du Plessis, provided the ingredients of this magnificent win. To be involved, in a small way, in such an event was the ultimate honour and joy.

I cannot recall a sporting event of any nature which has galvanised a nation in the way the World Cup has done. It has united South Africans irrespective of their colour, religion or political affiliation. What started as a minority spectator sport has ended up with 45 million devotees. The feat of the 15-odd players has given the nation the belief that success can be achieved against all the odds, through hard work and perseverance.

Perhaps the greatest achievement, though, is reserved for the game itself. The significance of Nelson Mandela wearing the Springbok jersey goes beyond a symbolic act of support for the team from a charismatic president. It ultimately signifies the acceptance of rugby football as the game of the new South Africa.

The Rugby World Cup board of directors. Back row (left to right): Nic Labuschagne, Leo Williams, Colin Jones; front row, Marcel Martin, Sir Ewart Bell, Keith Rowlands.

Leo Williams.

Though in its infancy, the RWC has established itself as one of the biggest events in international sport. To be honest, although the event is getting bigger by the year, it has yet to fulfil its enormous potential. In the eight years since the RWC concept was first tested in New Zealand and Australia, rugby has skyrocketed in status and popularity around the world. Unquestionably, the impetus of this revolution is the World Cup. It has become the yardstick by which the nations of the world measure their progress and ambitions.

It is important to remember that the 1995 tournament in South Africa, no matter how glamorous and spectacular, was only the tip of the iceberg. Fifty-three of the 67 members of the IB entered the competition. Of these, 44 countries were involved in the qualifying rounds. I attended qualifying tournaments in the Netherlands in 1993 and in Malaysia in 1994. Each was in fact a mini-World Cup in itself, and excellently organised by the host union. The passion and commitment of the participants, players, coaches and referees matched those of the 16 finalists, which speaks volumes about the international significance of the tournament. It is still early days, but I am certain that the World Cup will ultimately alter the international rugby landscape.

The 1995 event will be remembered as a landmark in the history of the game. It has rewritten the record books in terms of commercial success, attendances, numbers of TV viewers, quality matches and moments of excellence. It provided passionate, at times magnificent, battles and has launched a constellation of new stars on planet rugby. The only setback of this great celebration of sporting endeavour was the tragic injury, in a freak accident, to the Ivorian winger Max Brito.

South Africa deservedly won the tournament but the psychological edge of having a united nation and, specifically, President Mandela behind them should not be underestimated. In retrospect, they were a bit lucky to beat France, but their magnificent defensive effort against New Zealand in the final deserves full praise. My own country, Australia, obviously missed their cue. It was clear from the first game that something was not quite right. In the end we were deservedly beaten. In terms of preparation we could not have done more for the team, but now it is time for reassessment. We have to take a hard look at our priorities and the new developments in the game, and we must move forward.

I guess this sort of post-mortem is likely to happen with all the defeated senior teams: England, France, New Zealand, Wales and Ireland. Ultimately everybody has to start planning for 1999, and this is the challenge of the World Cup. As soon as one tournament is over, the next one looms large on the horizon. The king is dead, long live the king! Planning a new World Cup takes time and effort. The IB has decided to enlarge the tournament from 16 to 20 nations. This is an increase of 20 per cent. The board has also decided that only four teams will automatically qualify for 1999: South Africa, New Zealand, France and Wales. That is obviously going to dramatically alter the qualifying pattern. It means involving in the qualifying rounds teams like Australia, England, Western Samoa, Canada and Ireland, to mention just a few. We are aware of the difference in standards between the senior nations and the developing world and are trying to avoid mismatches. The qualifying rounds for the 1999 World Cup are already on the drawing board, while the 1997 RWC Sevens is in the early stages of planning. The world of rugby goes on.

SPOT THE DIFFERENCE!

They might look the same but the ball on the left is full of innovative ideas, like being made of a material that makes it easier to handle when wet. It's the same with vehicle auction companies. They might all look the same from the outside but

ADT Auctions is the world's largest auction group and all its resources are dedicated to helping their customers win. Whether you are buying or selling, ADT Auctions can provide the services, the venues and the products to suit you.

Best wishes from one great team to the others.

ADT *Auctions*

THE WORLD'S LARGEST AUCTION GROUP

AN ADT COMPANY

The Opening Ceremony
The rainbow nation welcomes the world
Nigel Starmer-Smith

The opening day of the 1995 Rugby World Cup was the realisation of a dream for South Africa. The rainbow nation came together in its full panoply of diverse colour, race and creed to provide an unforgettable ceremony to inaugurate the greatest sporting event ever staged in the country. Nor did the rugby match that followed it disappoint. It was a privilege just to be there. I was not alone in thinking that my visit to the World Cup would have been worthwhile had it been for this day alone. It would have been no surprise if the opening ceremony had overshadowed all else – its creation was inspired, the performance inspirational. South Africa owes a huge debt of gratitude to the designer and choreographer Neil McKay of the Razzle Dazzle Dance Company, and project co-ordinators Pro Touch Promotions.

This was the first public occasion on which it could be said that the whole of the Republic became visibly united. While nothing can conceal the stark contrast between the living conditions of the different communities in South Africa (for, unlike political transformation, significant economic and educational change necessarily takes decades, not days) the opening day of the World Cup seemed to symbolise, if only superficially, a new, common national identity. Who would have imagined a couple of years ago that a crowd comprising whites, blacks and coloureds would be chanting 'Nelson! Nelson!' as one upon President Mandela's almost Messianic arrival on the pitch at Newlands for his opening address? Who would have thought that the black community would ever be heard chanting 'Bokke! Bokke!' in support of an all-white South African national rugby XV? Every previous overseas visiting team had enjoyed the enthusiastic support of the non-white element in any rugby crowd. Here, though, was the new South Africa proudly extolling its 'one team, one nation' slogan – a country in patriotic ferment.

The opening ceremony was dripping with emotion as all strands of a multi-cultural society blended in

Nelson Mandela's Opening Speech

Sir Ewart Bell, guests of honour, players and supporters:

For the next 30 days, youth from the world's leading rugby nations will be displaying the finesse of a sport that provides entertainment and touches the hearts of hundreds of millions across the globe.

Your presence in South Africa affirms the unity in diversity, and the humanity in healthy contest, that our young democracy has come to symbolise.

On behalf of our rainbow nation, I welcome you all. We extend our hands across the miles to all rugby lovers who will be among us in spirit during this exciting period.

South Africa keenly appreciates your love and support. And we are grateful for the International Rugby Board's decision to hold this tournament here. It adds impetus to our own sports development programmes and, indeed, to our nation-building effort.

From the first kick-off, we are certain to witness rugby of an exceptional standard. Through it, we shall also contribute to the promotion of excellence, world peace and friendship.

South Africa opens its arms and its heart to embrace you all.

It is my privilege to declare this, the 1995 Rugby World Cup tournament, open.

flamboyant style. South Africa was publicly proclaiming a new age as the world looked on. The balance was brilliantly achieved in the opening moments of the pageant as the white, and white-uniformed, 55-piece South African Navy Band gave way to 150 Cape minstrels dressed in the colours of the new South African flag. The racial interplay continued with a troupe of 40 traditional Zulu dancers, a team of Gumboot dancers from the mine hostels and Mapantsula dancers from the Cape townships. The spectacular display of the ethnic diversity of the host country was represented by a further 600 performers from all corners of South Africa who, as gospel singer Jennifer Jones led the musical ensemble, combined to form a giant human map of the country.

More than 400 children of every colour ended the tableau by forming the words 'South Africa welcomes Rugby World Cup 1995'. Each participating nation was welcomed by national flag-bearers and children wearing the traditional costume of that country accompanied by its official rugby anthem.

All this was a prelude to the stunning performance of the Rugby World Cup anthem, 'World in Union', performed by rock star P.J. Powers; the symbolic lap of honour around the pitch, made by white former Springbok Danie Gerber and black player Irvin October; the welcome speech from Sir Ewart Bell, chairman of Rugby World Cup, and finally the opening words of Nelson Mandela – all the ingredients of a very special and moving occasion. One could only reflect on what a far cry all this was from the tawdry, feeble effort that passed for an opening ceremony at Twickenham in 1991.

What followed served to enhance the glad feeling that the Fates had conspired to ensure that this would be South Africa's day. The sun shone, the capacity crowd revelled in the pageant, and, of course, the Springboks beat the Wallabies, the reigning world champions, to crown an unprecedented day of joy for the host nation.

Get the basics right

NEXT

Pool A
The fairytale begins
Nigel Starmer-Smith

At 3.30 p.m. on Thursday 25 May, Welsh referee Derek Bevan, who had taken charge of the 1991 World Cup final, blew the whistle to get the 1995 event underway. As the advertisment hoardings from the Kruger Park to Cape Town had announced in letters writ large alongside a giant head-and-shoulders photograph of the coloured Springbok Chester Williams, South Africa's newest sporting hero – 'The Waiting's Over!' In fact the late withdrawal through a hamstring injury of wing threequarter Williams just ten days before the opening match had been a setback to South Africa – not to mention to the advertising campaigns of event sponsors VISA and South African Airways, who had made him the focal point for the propagation of the worldwide image of the 'new' South Africa and multi-racial Springbok rugby. It was a cruel blow to all to be deprived of the one non-white player in the Springbok squad selected entirely on merit. This was not the only hiccup. While most of the other preparatory celebrations went to plan – such as the nationwide promotional project of taking the World Cup ceremonial rugby ball by relay through the townships of the country from the Zulu *kraals* of Natal to the Khayelitsha and Guguletu communities of Cape Town – the official tournament welcome lunch for the 416 players of the 16 finalist nations, held in a giant marquee at the Groot Constantia Estate, was literally almost blown apart by torrential rain and wind in the Cape. The weather was also responsible for a long and (in the case of Ireland, Wales and New Zealand in particular) uncomfortable day's turbulent air travel for many of the teams who attended. As the team captains gathered together a little awkwardly for a group photograph, one couldn't help but wonder whether the topic of conversation amongst leading players might be of professional contracts and recruitment to some rugby tournament other than this World Cup.

More comforting was the announcement by the South African Rugby Football Union (SARFU) that 40 per cent of its share of World Cup profits would go towards a 6 million-rand drive to improve rugby facilities in underprivileged areas. Not for the last time during this event did one's thoughts drift back to the question of what had become of the profits – and of what measure were they? – of the two previous World Cups.

Late injury scares to Springbok captain François Pienaar and Wallaby Jason Little did not ultimately prevent both teams from fielding as intended their near strongest line-up for the opener, although the miraculous return to international rugby of Australia's Tim Horan was deferred for one further week to allow him the maximum possible time to regain full fitness after a knee injury sustained exactly one year earlier which had threatened to cripple him for life. So it was that ten of Australia's 1991 World Cup squad – eight of whom had competed in the 1991 final – took the field against a South African side whose combined number of international appearances amounted to 126, some 31 caps fewer than Australia's Michael Lynagh and David Campese had accumulated between them. The Springboks' lack of experience was, not surprisingly, a principal reason why many rugby 'experts' suggested that Australia entered the fray as marginal favourites to beat them. No one had allowed quite sufficiently for the home advantage and inspiration that was to be provided by the occasion as the crowd on this, South Africa's most famous day, celebrated and confirmed the country's final return from sporting isolation.

Joel Stransky, the South African fly-half, crosses the line to extend his side's lead against Australia.

Joost van der Westhuizen, given the perfect platform from his pack, sets the backs in motion.

After the toss of a coin – the 1921 florin used to start the 1925 international between England and the All Blacks – and a blast from Derek Bevan on a rugby whistle first blown in 1905, Michael Lynagh set the 1995 World Cup rolling.

Amid a cacophony of sound, the opening exchanges were frenetic and the Springbok support fanatical. That evening the T-shirt said it all. So, too, did the giant banner strung across the approach to Cape Town Airport, which read, quite simply, '27–18'. For South Africa, two tries, one conversion, four penalties and a dropped goal to Australia's two tries, one conversion and two penalty goals.

The bare statistics conceal the unrelenting excitement of a wonderful game which represented, as the next day's headlines were to couch it, the Springboks' finest hour. Lynagh's penalty, scored after an offside decision three minutes into the match, was countered three minutes later by a penalty goal for Joel Stransky after the Wallabies had dived over the ball in a ruck. It was to be the start of an especially memorable day for the 'home-town boy', a hero of Western Province, who was filling what had been considered the problem position of fly-half since the days of Naas Botha. Stransky's response to the challenge was worthy of Michael Lynagh at his best, cool and authoritative. On a day which saw the Australian captain uncharacteristically miss an early dropped goal and easy penalty chance, Stransky kicked for goal with aplomb.

Two more penalty kicks in reply to one from Lynagh put South Africa ahead for the first time after half an hour. The Springbok pack provided a platform, based on good

Pieter Hendriks, the late replacement for the injured Chester Williams, rounds David Campese to score South Africa's first try of the tournament.

loose ball, for the powerful Joost van der Westhuizen to display his range of footballing skills, sniping runs, lightning acceleration, intelligent kicks and a service much improved over the previous two years. As a belligerent back row outgunned Australia, only the work of John Eales in the line-out redressed the balance for the Wallabies. In fact, it was a sequence of superb rucks, five in a row, that set up Australia's first try, as for once the Springboks' defensive line evaporated and Lynagh strolled over.

With Van der Westhuizen and Stransky having gone tantalisingly close to crossing the Australian line and South Africa four points behind, the roar that greeted the try that turned the match round is probably still echoing around the gullies of Table Mountain. It was poetic justice for the scorer, left wing Pieter Hendriks, who must have felt more than anyone the impact of the nationwide expression of grief at the enforced absence from the Springbok team of Chester Williams. A counter-attack of typically exciting thrust and vision from full-back André Joubert, a burst by James Small, a feed on to James Dalton, a ruck and an inspired miss-move pass from Stransky set up Hendriks for a one-on-one challenge against David Campese. The robust left wing went outside Campo to score in the corner. South Africa were back in the lead and the crowd were ecstatic. There was no conversion – Stransky's only missed kick at goal – and as half-time came South Africa were ahead by 14–13. They had narrowly missed a chance to extend their lead when Van der Westhuizen just failed to hold a scoring pass from Stransky on the break With the change of ends, there was to be no turning back: the pattern did not change.

If line-out domination has been regarded as the surest foundation of victory, here was the contest to dismiss that hypothesis. Springboks Andrews and Strydom, hampered by Dalton's sometimes wayward throwing in, never challenged Eales' supremacy, but what they lacked in line-out ball they more than compensated for in ruck and maul. François Pienaar and Ruben Kruger were outstanding and the half-back pairing flourished behind them – in contrast to Australia's much-vaunted George Gregan, who found life in his fifth international a tough experience. South Africa's back row made sure of that. The Springboks continued to soak up the pressure as Tim Gavin and Willie Ofahengaue attacked close the scrum. Little and Herbert were felled time and again as South Africa's midfield stood firm. Seldom if ever did Australia

Rudolf Straeuli pounces on the loose ball with his captain, François Pienaar, in close attendance.

try to work the blind side, and Gregan's predictability, pass upon pass – no kick, no break, no back-row move – was manna from heaven for the Springbok defenders.

As South Africa stretched their lead with a Stransky penalty and dropped goal four minutes later, so their confidence and conviction grew. We awaited the world champions' response. It didn't happen until it was too late. At 20–13 ahead it was South Africa who continued to exert the pressure – and it was that pressure that was the key to their ultimate success. It led to the try that put them two scores clear 17 minutes from the end. From a 5-metre scrum No. 8 Rudolf Straeuli fed scrum-half Van der Westhuizen and the inside pass created the gap through which Stransky sped untouched. He rounded off his glory day with the conversion. How important, too, that conversion was. A lead of 15 points, as opposed to 13, allowed the home victory celebrations to start early.

Australia's response in the last quarter of an hour was as predictable and valiant as it was in vain. The Wallaby onslaught was finally rewarded with a try by Phil Kearns in a scramble on the Springbok line after a touch of adventure – a 'miss-three' pass by Lynagh in the build-up. But the urgency and commitment of those dying minutes arrived too late for Australia. The final whistle heralded not only a pitch invasion but a long night of unbridled celebration and lingering contentment in its aftermath.

Passion was the key to South Africa's success; a hunger to succeed that for so many years had been the prerogative of Wallaby and All Black teams. Morné du Plessis, the popular Springbok team manager, had been the calming influence on his players in the preceding days of hype and near-hysteria. The controversial regime of Kitch Christie, whose coaching emphasis was on a rigid

The South African coaching staff, Morné du Plessis and Kitch Christie, oversee their team's training session. They had been the subject of much criticism before the start of the tournament.

(some had called it spartan) training schedule with fitness at its core, had been vindicated.

Whatever was to follow the opening day, it was always going to be a case of 'after the Lord Mayor's Show' as far as the general public were concerned. Not for Canada, however. Their high hopes of going a long way in the 1995 World Cup had been based on a courageous and inspiring performance in 1991, which saw them beat Fiji and Romania, lose narrowly to France in their pool matches and give New Zealand a real scare before going down 13–29 in the quarter-final in Lille. Such were the Canadian expectations of success that when the draw put Canada alongside Australia and South Africa, together with Romania, the pool was immediately dubbed the 'group of death'. Victories over England (albeit an under-strength side in a non-cap match) in May 1993, Wales in Cardiff the following November and France in June 1994 gave some measure of credence to the idea that this was the toughest qualifying group of the four. Considering that the squad contained five survivors of the 1987 World Cup squad and 11 from 1991, spearheaded by a new captain, fly-half Gareth Rees, and forwards Gord MacKinnon, Al Charron and Glen Ennis, Rugby Canada's optimism appeared to have a solid basis. But an ambitious world tour which encompassed matches in the United Kingdom, France, South America, the South Sea Islands and New Zealand during the five months up to April 1995 served to put things in perspective. Of seven international matches only two were won – against Uruguay and Fiji – and the culmination was Canada's heaviest-ever defeat, 73–7 against New Zealand in Auckland. Together with the unfortunate personality clash between coach Ian Birtwell and former captain and cornerstone of the pack Norm Hadley, which resulted in the absence of Hadley from the World Cup squad, events had changed any objective assessment of the prospects for Canada quite dramatically. Not even their fresh, dynamic approach, typified by the spectacular multi-coloured Maple leaf strip, nor the team brochure cover, which read: 'Canadian National Team Wins (the word half-completed) 1995 Rugby World Cup. It can happen', could disguise the reality of the situation.

If Canada's hopes of creating a major upset looked slim, then Romania's seemed even slimmer. The preceding season had brought a succession of defeats: by Wales and Italy in the World Cup group qualifying matches, by England (54–3), France and Scotland. Romania's only success had been against Japan in one of two Tests. As ever, they left the sad impression of a cruelly disadvantaged rugby nation among the major powers: poorly resourced, undernourished, friendless, but oh-so-friendly and courteous themselves, living off the interest of the charitable fund, held in London, which was established by the RFU after the special international played at Twickenham before the Romanian political upheavals of 1991. It perturbed me greatly to learn that, as talk of multi-million-pound profits from Rugby World Cup was bandied around, Romania had yet to receive one penny of support for its rugby from that source. All credit to the South African squad this World Cup for their gesture in arranging the supply of some Adidas kit for the Romanians, who remain without sponsors.

Without realistic ambition, then, Romanian manager Theodor Radulescu freely admitted that he regarded their opening match with Canada as their World Cup final. The two nations had met just once before, in the pool match of the 1991 World Cup in Toulouse, when Canada's powerful pack had held sway to win 19–11. This time the setting was the superbly presented Boet Erasmus Stadium in Port Elizabeth, where one was reminded of the occasion 21 years before on which Willie John McBride had led the British Lions rampant to clinch the Test series 3–0 against South Africa. Now, on a beautiful balmy evening, lights shone out from the new hospitality boxes and the carriages behind the old steam train that forms an original backdrop to the length of the long open terrace opposite the main stand. There was an air of unreality surrounding proceedings, in stark contrast to the events at Newlands the previous afternoon. A crowd of about 20,000 interested but quiet onlookers included only a handful of partisan flag-waving Canadian supporters, and still fewer partisan Romanians.

It took a long time for Canada to establish their superiority. For 20 minutes there was huge endeavour but limited skill before a Canadian forward drive produced a try for prop forward Rod Snow, against the run of play. Romania's key points-scoring weapon, Neculai Nichitean (192 points in 23 internationals) had failed to turn good pressure into points, missing two early penalties. Snow's try marked the watershed and after their slow – battle-weary, it seemed – start, Canada proceeded to outclass the Romanians. A light drizzle added to the players' problems in a frenetic, error-strewn second quarter in which Gareth Rees kicked two penalty goals to one by Nichitean. The second half saw Canada get into the groove and eventually brush the East Europeans aside. The back row of Al Charron, Ian Gordon and Colin McKenzie re-emphasised Canada's continued world class in that sphere of the game and, with Glen Ennis, John Hutchinson and Gord MacKinnon in

reserve, ensured that back-row selection for the matches to follow was going to revolve around an embarrassment of riches. Behind the pack, quicksilver John Graf and Gareth Rees at half-back ran the show for the last 60 minutes, 19 points in all coming from the boot of Welsh Canadian Rees (four penalties, two conversions and a dropped goal). There were two further tries, one by Colin McKenzie, and, most memorably, a wide-ranging affair displaying sleight of hand and deft skills, involving the two Stewarts, full-back Scott and centre Christian; winger Dave Lougheed; Graf and the scorer himself, the outstanding Al Charron.

The 34–3 result represented a satisfactory performance for Canada and ensured that Australia could take nothing for granted in their next game, but Romania had done little to increase nervous tension in the Springbok camp. Lingering but contrasting questions remained for the two teams. For Canada there was an obvious problem in winning clean line-out ball (alas, no Hadley); for Romania there were fewer difficulties with set-piece play, but little ability in winning ball in the loose.

The euphoria that greeted the Springboks' triumph on the opening day at Newlands was soon to evaporate. Romania's approach to the game against the home nation had been nothing if not realistic. In the words of coach Mircea Paraschiv: 'Having lost to Canada, we have to confront two atomic bombs, like Nagasaki and Hiroshima: South Africa and Australia.' But Romania ended the day in song, not shell-shocked. As South Africa took the field for the first time ever against Romania there was a breeze blowing off Table Mountain, but that did not cool the ardour of 40,000 or so supporters as much as the erratic performance of the 'change' Springboks. It was not to be the day of celebration and landslide victory so many had expected. South Africa won, but the plaudits went to Romania. Having failed so dismally against Canada, they found renewed spirit and pride plus an excellent pair of young half-backs in Flutur and Ivanciuc. Their combined efforts came close to embarrassing the second-string Springboks, although the result itself was never really in doubt.

Adriaan Richter, understudy to François Pienaar as captain, must have thought his team was in for a comfortable afternoon of controlled rugby as first Gavin Johnson kicked a penalty and then he himself touched down a solid pushover for an 8–0 lead after ten minutes. But it was only in the set scrum that South Africa showed any real authority throughout, for despite their greater

Romanian scrum-half Vasile Flutur spins the ball away to his backs during his side's spirited performance against South Africa.

share of possession, the Springboks made too many errors, while the Romanians were fierce and committed in the tackle. For half-backs Johan Roux and Hennie le Roux it was an uncomfortable afternoon and that lack of fluency was largely responsible for preventing the centre pairing of Brendan Venter and Christian Scholtz from penetrating the midfield. Fortunately for South Africa, Romania failed to capitalise on some good loose ball and at half-time the score remained 8–0. In a near-repeat of the first-half sequence, Gavin Johnson kicked a second penalty goal following an offside infringement before, reverting to basics, the Springbok pack set up a massive forward drive following a high kick and Richter touched down for a second try. Johnson's conversion and a further penalty goal by him put South Africa comfortably ahead. A solitary early penalty goal by Ivanciuc was Romania's scant reward. Yet the final quarter of the match was all about the determination of Romania to restore lost pride, and happily it was they who were to score the best try of the game, three minutes from the end. After a tremendous

counter-attack by full-back Vasile Brici and a clever switch with scrum-half Flutur, wing forward Andrei Guranescu crashed over for a well-earned try. With the final score of 21–8 Romania knew that their chance of progressing in the tournament was as good as over, but in giving South Africa – recently installed as World Cup favourites – a difficult afternoon they had achieved their limited objective of proving their worth as a participant in the finals. As for South Africa, as manager Morné du Plessis was to put it, 'We have taken a knock, it's a comeback to earth for us and might be a good thing. We won, we got three points, and whatever the score today, we would still have to beat Canada.' The subdued response of the home crowd at Newlands spoke volumes, however.

But if South Africa were feeling temporarily out of sorts that was nothing compared to Australia's discomfiture. From the moment Mark Andrews had secured the ball for South Africa from Michael Lynagh's kick-off in the opening game, little had gone right. As Bob Dwyer reflected between matches, there had been fundamental errors by the Wallabies, such as retaining possession only once from the 14 kick-offs contested – errors compounded by a lack of urgency, an apparent lack of enthusiasm and a lack of forward momentum. There was an acerbic edge to Dwyer's post-match observations, and when he announced that the team selection for the match with Canada would include all the squad members who had not taken part in the opening game – 'They deserve their chance to show they can do better' – there was no concealing his disappointment and irritation at the 'first XV's' below-par performance. But even as Australia rang the changes, a former World Cup hero of 1991, Troy Coker, was forced to withdraw from the tournament with persistent hamstring trouble. However, the inclusion of Tim Horan confirmed his miraculous recovery from an appalling injury suffered a year previously while he was playing for Queensland in the Super-10 final against Natal. It marked the reunion of the world's best centre partnership with Jason Little, for the first Test match since Australia played France in Paris in November 1993.

In three previous meetings Canada had been swamped – most recently by 43–16 in Calgary in 1993. This was also the moment of truth for both sides. To survive to the quarter-finals, each knew they had to win. The stakes, and the tensions, in Port Elizabeth were high. Canada never recovered from an opening 11-minute Wallaby whirlwind, a swift response from the world champions to the shortcomings of their opening game with South Africa. It was an onslaught that was later to be mirrored by New Zealand in cutting England down to size in the semi-final in Cape Town. This was some instant backlash: there were two tries, two conversions and a penalty goal for Australia before Canada had scarcely touched the ball. It was a quite brilliant spell which captivated the crowd of 18,000, whose instinctive support of the underdog was to help lift Canada in their subsequent rearguard action. But initially it was the revamped Australian pack that ruled the roost and Michael Lynagh was back to striking the ball in his accustomed style. He kicked the penalty goal and converted both tries, the first by Ilie Tabua, and then, at the end of a slick threequarter movement, one from wing

Michael Lynagh registers his second try of the tournament against Canada.

Joe Roff, Australia's burly 19-year-old newcomer, the nearest equivalent in any other team to the star of the tournament, All Black Jonah Lomu. Yet that Wallaby purple patch rather flattered to deceive, and it was really the only spell of complete Australian authority. A Canadian resurgence brought two Gareth Rees penalties before Lynagh replied with one for Australia to make it 20–6 at half-time.

The last 40 minutes brought a comparatively even battle of cut and thrust. A neat touch of class from Lynagh gave him a try, which he also converted, before Canada, compensating in loose-ball possession for what they were losing in the line-out to John Eales and the back-row men, made tremendous inroads with their use of second-phase ball. They played fast and loose; one sensed that all that was lacking were the clinical finishing skills. Time and again the trio of Charron, MacKinnon and Hutchinson challenged Australia and put immense pressure on their defence. Eventually Al Charron made it to the line for an unconverted try – a just reward. But 27–11 to Australia was how it stayed until the end amid a valiant display by the North Americans, typified by the moment the Port

David Campese hands off his opposite number, the Canadian Winston Stanley.

Elizabeth crowd enjoyed most of all, when winger Winston Stanley brought the flying David Campese down to earth with a bang to save a certain try. It summed up Canada's brave but unavailing effort. For Australia it was an essential win, but with injuries to Hartill, Kearns and Slattery, and, the first ten minutes excepted, a lack of forward control, many doubts about their performance lingered.

Three days later the Wallabies were in action again, facing Romania for the first time ever in the first Test match to be played at the new redeveloped Danie Craven Stadium at Stellenbosch, situated just 40 kilometres away from Cape Town against the backcloth of the Hottentot Mountains. There can be few more magnificent settings in the world for a rugby match. On yet another gloriously sunny midwinter's day, Australia took the field in gold and green hooped jerseys – a first change of strip in 35 years – having lost the toss to retain the normal jersey in a gold–yellow clash with Romania. The Romanians were a more buoyant outfit in the aftermath of their spirited display against South Africa. For Australia, apart from the obvious need to win, there was the added incentive to score as many points – or rather, tries – as possible. If Canada were to beat South Africa later that day, Australia could still top the pool ahead of South Africa on the try count – and thus avoid England, likely winners of Pool B, in the quarter-final. Not that a very physical Western Samoan team were looking particularly inviting alternative opponents for the runners-up in this pool.

Despite a convincing margin of victory (42–3) at the end of the game, there was still no great conviction about Australia's performance. Former World Cup-winning captain Nick Farr-Jones remained bemused. 'The hunger is still missing. Is it that having drunk once from the Cup you lose a bit of the thirst? Or is it that the advent of the Super League brings the promise of rich pickings for many, and when someone knows his financial future is secure, does he continue to perform at the same level?' Certainly John Eales could not be faulted, and his eventual domination of the line-out, alongside an improved showing from Rod McCall, formed the cornerstone of Australia's victory once they had subdued Romania's first-half-hour assault. Would that Romania had had the firepower behind the scrum to match the commitment of Cojocariu and Ciorascu in the forward exchanges and the repeated second-phase raids from the back row – and this despite conceding more than 18lb per man to the Australian pack. For 30 minutes the Romanians bothered the Australian defence, but their reward for a wealth of possession was a solitary dropped goal by the newly elevated fly-half, Ivanciuc.

Having weathered the storm, the Wallabies took control. Surging attacks saw tries before half-time from Michael Foley and then Joe Roff, with a swerve inside, then outside the last defender after a superb sweep through the middle by Damian Smith. Without Lynagh's presence, the place-kicking was proving a problem for Australia, with a lone conversion to show from six kicks at goal. So when Roff added a powerful second try soon after half-time, following an Eales drive upfield and a clever turn pass by Herbert, who should step up to convert the goal? None other than John Eales, whose international points-scoring record comprised, until this moment, one try. Nonetheless Eales revealed rather more style than renowned Scotland forward and place-kicker Peter Brown as he proceeded to put over four conversions in a row, Burke, Damian Smith and finally the dynamic flanker David Wilson running in three more tries for an emphatic, if not entirely convincing win. 'We're heading in the right direction,' said Bob Dwyer afterwards. That was about the sum of this display. The outcome of the pool, and who would qualify first and second, therefore rested excitingly with South Africa and the credible challenge of Canada in the climax to the group games. The focus of attention that same evening was once again was on Port Elizabeth. No one could have anticipated what lay in store.

The Canadians knew the magnitude of the task ahead. This was do or die. In their first-ever meeting with South Africa, Canada needed to win and to score at least one more try than their opponents to achieve the 'unthinkable' – at least from a South African point of view – by ousting the Springboks and joining Australia in the quarter-finals. There was plenty at stake, then, and more than enough tension surrounding the encounter even before the remarkable turn of events that was to cast a pall over the occasion.

As the 8 p.m. kick-off time approached the Boet Erasmus Stadium was half obscured by the dense, pungent smoke from a hundred *braaiis* that wafted across the field from adjacent car parks. For South Africa, François Pienaar was back at the helm, leading just six of the side that had started out against Australia; ten of the team from the Romania match. There was still concern about line-out capability, and worry too over the fitness, and late withdrawal, of James Small. Canada, putting an

Romanian lock forward Sandu Ciorascu leaps above the other players to win possession for his team. The game saw Australia play in a different strip for the first time in 35 years. It had no effect on them, however, as they coasted home to a 42–3 victory.

emphasis on mobility and recognising their strength in depth in the back row, had moved Al Charron up to the second row to try to bolster a definite weak area, and kept 11 of the team that had battled hard against Australia.

The taut-faced teams took to the field on this cool, yet strangely muggy evening; the anthems played, the players took up their positions and, just as the signal was given to Irish referee David McHugh to start the match, the floodlights failed. Thankfully, the stadium was not completely bereft of light because, according to one possibly mischievous source (the facts have not been confirmed), the power for the floodlights came from temporary generators brought in by Rugby World Cup, rather than the normal supply that serves the whole of Port Elizabeth. Certainly the local electricity board continued to supply the hospitality boxes, press areas and stadium buildings while the pitch area remained unlit.

The presence of the background lighting was fortuitous. Indeed, without it things might have become frightening and threatening on the open terraces holding a crowd of 30,000 or more. Eventually, despite the deafening silence of the public address system, news leaked through that a cable had been severed and repairs were being undertaken. Police helicopters circled above, their searchlights adding to the incongruity of the extraordinary scene below. The players, back in the dressing rooms, waited for news; so, too, did the crowd. The tournament and stadium officials, referee and team

Kobus Wiese soars to take a line-out ball in the ill-tempered game against Canada.

management personnel discussed what was to be done. The World Cup regulations stated that if a match was not started within 20 minutes of the official kick-off time, the game was to be declared abandoned and the points obtaining to be shared. This would have given two points to each team, making South Africa top qualifiers with eight points, Australia runners-up with seven, leaving Canada, on six, to exit the tournament with Romania. Happily, Springbok manager Morné du Plessis wanted none of that, although, like his Canadian counterpart, Ray Skett, he insisted that his players be given a definite time by which the lights could be fixed and the start rescheduled. Eventually, a kick-off time of 8.45 p.m. was announced, and at 8.47 the World Cup match that nearly never happened, began. In some ways it might have been better if it had not.

After a tricky waiting period for the teams, nerves must have been more than usually frayed and the refocusing on the task in hand exceptionally difficult. Early exchanges brought chances to both teams – a missed drop-goal attempt by Stransky; a fine break by Christian Stewart wasted by a forward pass. But it was the Springboks who remained the more composed and efficient in a game that was ruthless from the start. It was obvious that Canada were going to be no pushover, but South Africa's two tries were; both touched down by No. 8 Adriaan Richter as his pack took control in the tight. All the ingenuity in the world, and all Canada's incredible tenacity, could not compensate for the superior Springbok power up front and the pushover tries served to emphasise the contrast in forward strengths. Canada, at times living on mere scraps of possession, ran everything, and ran it fast, but they could not retain the ball long enough to breach an impeccable defence. South Africa's set-piece play kept them secure, and with two Stransky penalty goals to add to two converted tries, their 20–0 lead looked impregnable. But Canada, who had been building up to this climactic day virtually since their exit from the 1991 World Cup, were never going to concede defeat, and the Springboks, each of them hell-bent on winning a team place for the final rounds, were never going to ease up. The ingredients for disaster were there for all to see as the tension mounted; the impact frightening in some helter-skelter passages in the second half; the explosion almost inevitable as an unyielding South African defence was assailed by an unrelenting Canadian effort.

It came with seven minutes remaining, a free-for-all sparked by an unpleasant confrontation in a wingers' clash between Pieter Hendriks and Winston Stanley. It was unpleasant, but something that would have fizzled out in a game less charged with emotion. Indeed, the crisis moment might still have passed but for the headstrong action of Canadian full-back Scott Stewart, who charged

South Africa's James Dalton and Canada's Gareth Rees and Rod Snow receive their marching orders from referee David McHugh.

into the fray and precipitated the all-out battle. Fists flew as tempers were lost. The lid was off the boiling pot, and, unforgivably, even a boot was launched in anger. The situation was as unenviable as it was impossible for referee McHugh as he consulted touch-judge Stephen Hilditch. McHugh could have sent off half a dozen or more players or even abandoned the game. He settled on three to receive their marching orders – and none was an innocent party. James Dalton, warned earlier in the game, Canadian captain Gareth Rees and prop Rod Snow left the field for an early bath. The mass brawl and dismissals cast a cloud over this sporting showpiece. South Africa duly topped the table and Canada were out of the Cup – but on a night like that few objective onlookers cared very much either way. Despite pleas from the Springbok camp, James Dalton received a 30-day suspension and an end to his World Cup dreams, while Rees and Snow did not bother to contest their punishment, confirmed by the match commissioner present, Ray Williams. For them the World Cup was over anyway. Nor was that the end of the matter. On further perusal of the video of the match, the Rugby World Cup directors cited both Pieter Hendriks, for kicking, and Scott Stewart, for punching and being an originator of the incident. Each was suspended, and for Hendriks, the player hailed as South Africa's try-scoring

hero in the opening match, the glory days were over. But even such personal disasters were quickly put into perspective when news broke of the appalling injury to Ivory Coast player Max Brito, paralysed for life after an injury sustained in the final match in Pool D.

For South Africa there was a twist to the tale: Hendriks' departure opened the door for the return to the fold of the injured folk hero Chester Williams, thanks to a curious regulation that allowed a suspended player to be replaced in the squad. Sponsors VISA and South African Airways must have had some premonition. For Williams and his army of adoring fans, the fairytale was about to unfold. And as the Springboks counted the cost to their campaign of suspensions and injuries, the squad regrouped in anticipation of meeting the physical challenge of Western Samoa in the quarter-finals.

The disgraced Canadian pairing both received 30-day bans, but for them the World Cup was already over.

Australia, meanwhile, yet to hit top form, had to settle for their day of destiny in a repeat of the 1991 World Cup final against England. Canada left beaten but unbowed, ambition unfulfilled, while Romania were content that they had had their say. In all it was a fascinating story within a story.

FOUR TO CARRY ME HOME

The Official Beer of the England Rugby Squad

Pool B
England's shaky start
Ian Robertson

Since England lost the previous World Cup final to Australia on 2 November 1991, they have been far and away the most successful country in the northern hemisphere. There have been two Grand Slams in the Five Nations Championship, in 1992 and 1995, and two major scalps in between with victories over New Zealand in 1993 at Twickenham and against South Africa in 1994 in Pretoria. At the outset of the World Cup they fully deserved to be quoted by leading bookmakers Ladbrokes at 4–1, right behind the 5–2 joint favourites, Australia and South Africa. After all, they arrived in South Africa with a mighty impressive record of six straight wins in succession. Admittedly, they had scarcely needed to move out of second gear to beat Romania and Canada before Christmas, but in the first three months of 1995 they went on to prove in the most decisive manner that they were the best team in Europe by a considerable margin. Turbo-charged and nuclear-powered, they won the Five Nations at a canter and hopes were very high that they would hit the ground running when they landed in Durban and unceremoniously sweep away all opposition in Pool B.

Yet not for the first time in my 25 years covering international rugby for the BBC, England flattered to deceive. As so often before when much has been expected of them, they failed to deliver. In all three pool matches they spent long periods trying to scale the heights of mediocrity, and certainly against Argentina and Italy, they never even managed to achieve lift-off from base. Far from shinning up Everest, they were scampering round the foothills like headless chickens. Any resemblance between England in Durban and World Cup champions was purely coincidental and hardly discernible. But the fact remains that they won all three of their pool matches, which no other Home Union team managed, an achievement equalled only by New Zealand, South Africa and France.

On the face of it, this should have been a perfect group for England, because they faced three reasonably good sides, all of whom could be expected to give them a decent game without ever really threatening to defeat them. In theory that sort of challenge is the ideal build-up to the quarter-final stage; it is certainly preferable to the facile and totally irrelevant landslide victories of the kind New Zealand enjoyed over Japan (145–17) or Scotland had over the Ivory Coast (89–0). Everything, then, bode well for England. They were drawn with three teams all good enough to provide worthwhile opposition but each 30 points behind the Five Nations Grand Slam champions.

So what went wrong? The answer is simple – England failed to reproduce anything remotely near their Five Nations form against Argentina and Italy and only recaptured their best rugby in the first half of the Western Samoan match. The most frustrating aspect of all this was the fact that no one before, during or after that fortnight in Durban could come up with an explanation for this sudden lapse. The players were all phenomenally fit, trained to the peak and surrounded by a plethora of support men ranging from doctor, physiotherapist, psychologist and dietician to two of the best coaches in world rugby in Jack Rowell and Les Cusworth. Even the playing conditions were stacked in England's favour. Not for them the usual Natal midday temperature of 80 degrees with its accompanying humidity. Their first two games were at five o'clock in the evening under floodlights and the third was at eight o'clock in the evening.

Furthermore, a cursory glance at the individual talents in the four teams in Pool B was enough to underline the indisputable fact that the English players were in a different class. They alone had three giant locks – in Martin Bayfield, Martin Johnson and Richard West – two of them only a couple of inches short of 7ft and Johnson a commanding 6ft7. The other three countries had no single loose forward able to compete in the line-out against any one of England's three first-choice players: Ben Clarke, Dean Richards and Tim Rodber. Add to that a solid, formidable front row and England's renowned strength in the maul and it is easy to appreciate why they were expected to cruise through to the quarter-final.

There is no doubt they had the best all-round pack of forwards, but what should have been even more significant was that they had a back division positively bristling with world-class talent, which should have been able to cut loose and run riot against Argentina, Italy and Western Samoa. They also had the best two scrum-halves in the pool in Dewi Morris and Kyran Bracken, and the best fly-half, Rob Andrew. In the whole World Cup only Australia could boast a centre partnership in the same league as Will Carling and Jeremy Guscott, and Phil de Glanville was only a whisker behind these two great players. With the flying Underwood brothers to inject real pace and power on the wings and the added bonus of an exciting running full-back in Mike Catt, it is not surprising that there were huge expectations of this English side.

Not that the other teams were exactly bereft of talent themselves. The Italians had three backs who all caught the eye at various stages of the tournament. Paolo Vaccari displayed his versatility by playing with equal confidence at full-back and on the wing; Ivan Francescato, who was outstanding at scrum-half in the 1991 World Cup, proved a very elusive runner at centre threequarter and Diego Dominguez performed with great skill and composure at fly-half. Up front, the skipper, Massimo Cuttitta, was a decent prop and Mark Giacheri confirmed his potential as a genuine line-out forward. Italy also had a couple of good loose forwards in former Australian No. 8 Julian

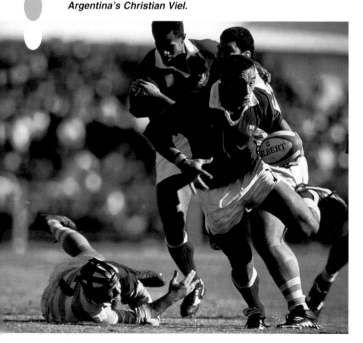

Junior Paramore, the outstanding Western Samoan flanker, breaks the tackle of Argentina's Christian Viel.

Gardner and flanker Orazio Arancio.

It is more difficult to single out Argentinian forwards because their pack is a collective unit, but both flankers, Christian Viel and Rolando Martin, were very productive in the loose. Their backs lacked a real cutting edge although most of them were reasonable footballers.

Western Samoa were like Argentina in that the sum of the individual parts posed much more of a threat than the individuals themselves. Having said that, they had one flanker, Peter Junior Paramore, who would certainly have been up to Five Nations international rugby and two very talented wings, Brian Lima and George Harder.

But if you had thrown the top 15 players from each of the four countries in this pool into a lucky bag and then chosen the best composite side, it is more than likely that the whole England XV would have been picked en bloc. An argument could be made for selecting the entire Argentinian front row for their remarkable set-piece play and Junior Paramore might deserve to be picked as an openside flanker, but, man for man, England looked better than the other three countries put together. Such a state of affairs would certainly not have been the case in any of the other three World Cup pools.

It is against this background that England should be judged, and unfortunately, in their performances in the first two matches they fell a long way short of the very high standards they had set themselves. They arrived in Durban bubbling with confidence following their nine-month unbeaten run. In stark contrast, their first opponents, Argentina, had lost four of their previous six internationals, albeit in South Africa and Australia. They conceded 171 points in those four games, and England were expected to match the average score of over 40 points against them, including a few tries.

In the event, England won 24–18 without scoring a try. To be fair, they were not helped by the conditions. After a week of blue sky and sunshine, a tropical downpour greeted the teams in the first half. The rain undoubtedly upset England's plans, but not nearly as much as the remarkably powerful Argentinian scrummaging did. It has to be said that while there were many divergent views on who was the best player of the tournament, which was the best unseeded team or which was the best try, virtually everyone was in agreement that the Pumas had the best scrummage. They have perfected their own technique of an eight-man shove to an art form and they are able to inconvenience and embarrass any and every side in the world in this specialist area. They are capable of driving forward on their own put-in, where they don't even bother to strike for the ball, and also on

Rob Andrew, England's fly-half, kept his side in the game against Argentina with six penalties and two dropped goals.

the opposition put-in. England found this most disconcerting and gave credence to the old adage that if a team is disrupted in the set scrums, their control in general play often disintegrates.

Considering the heights England had reached in the Five Nations and were to scale in their quarter-final victory over Australia, one can only assume that they thought a 100 per cent effort would not be needed to beat Argentina. The painful truth is that if the Pumas had had a reliable goal-kicker they would almost certainly have won. Fly-half Lisandro Arbizu missed half a dozen opportunities, including one drop at goal and one conversion, and it was only Rob Andrew's six penalties from six attempts, and two dropped goals from three attempts, that made the difference between the teams at the end. England's saving grace, apart from Rob Andrew's magnificent kicking exhibition, was their overwhelming superiority in the line-out, and here there were outstanding displays from locks Martin Bayfield and Martin Johnson with excellent support at the back, where Ben Clarke, Tim Rodber and Steve Ojomoh dwarfed their opponents.

There was a time in the 1970s and 1980s when England were quite content to beat emerging nations reasonably narrowly rather than put them to the sword as the All Blacks have always done. In the past few years, though, they have adopted a more clinical and ruthless approach to international rugby and in the World Cup season they destroyed Romania by 54–3 and Canada by 60–19. Had they reproduced their Grand Slam form, I have no doubt they would have rattled up 40 or 50 points against Argentina and Italy but instead they fell from grace with a resounding thump.

Of course, as every schoolboy knows, you do not suddenly become a bad side overnight and inside this very disappointing effort were 15 highly trained and highly talented athletes waiting to explode into action and show the world just how good they really were. To their great credit they admitted quite openly after the match that this was one of their poorest performances for a decade. They could have argued that they led 12–0 at half-time; that they did only as much as they had to do and were never in any real danger of losing. But when you are one of the top three sides in world rugby, you can afford the luxury of self-criticism. On the basis that it is not possible to peak for every single match in a ten-month period featuring 12 internationals, it makes sense to save the very best efforts for the very best sides and the odd trough or plateau for the world's less exalted countries such as Argentina and Italy.

Rob Andrew kept England in the driving seat with four

penalties in the first half. He further eased the situation with an excellent dropped goal and a fifth penalty in the first ten minutes of the second half. Crexell replied with a penalty for Argentina and then, a quarter of an hour into the second half, Noriega, the Pumas' tight-head prop, thundered over for a try which Arbizu converted. Andrew added his second dropped goal only to see Arbizu land his first penalty to narrow the gap to eight points with fifteen minutes left. Andrew knocked over one last penalty, but the momentary relief of the English supporters in the crowd evaporated when Arbizu side-stepped through some rather indifferent tackling to score a neat try. Argentina were only one score away from creating a major upset, but England held on to win by six points.

England's captain, Will Carling, leaves the field after suffering ankle damage against Argentina.

As so often, Andrew was the star of the show for his exceptional kicking as well as a splendid display at fly-half. Dewi Morris had an extremely good game at scrum-half, but regrettably the rest of England's multi-talented back line posed very little threat to a sturdy, determined Argentinian defence. There was a feeling that perhaps we had expected too much from England. After all, this was their first game together for well over two months, and

several members of the team had played precious little rugby in that time. What is more, Argentina played to their full potential and that proved their bold effort against Australia three weeks earlier had been no fluke. The optimists claimed that England had won playing badly and that, they argued, was often the hallmark of a good team. The sceptics needed convincing, but we were assured that everything would fall into place against Italy in the next match. We didn't all fall for that explanation, especially as the Italians had beaten Ireland three weeks previously, but it still seemed a reasonable bet that England would demolish Italy in 1995 just as they had done at Twickenham in the 1991 World Cup. The score that day was 36–6, and the critics anticipated a similar winning margin in Durban.

As it transpired, England won by only seven points, and it has to be said that they were almost as unconvincing in this match as they had been against Argentina. But rather than slate England, I should pay tribute to the Italians, who have made giant strides in recent years and are unquestionably a far better balanced side now than they were in 1991. Their record in the past 12 months speaks volumes. In June 1994 they lost narrowly to the then world champions, Australia, in Brisbane by 23–20 and in Sydney by 20–7.

In their World Cup qualifying match in Cardiff, they lost by only 29–19 to Wales and then, just three weeks before the start of the World Cup in South Africa, they beat Ireland 22–12. There is no doubt that Italy are now a major force in European rugby and on the world stage, and they are bound to continue to push very hard in the near future to be given regular fixtures against the Home Unions in the fervent hope of eventually being included in a Six Nations Championship.

One key factor in the improvement in Italian rugby has been the excellent work of the new coach, Georges Coste. This French-born former scrum-half achieved success with Perpignan in the French first division, and in the 18 months since he became national coach of Italy he has transformed their play. He has brought defensive organisation and tactical discipline to the side and in extracting the best from a talented group of players he has instilled a confidence and self-belief which was embarrassingly lacking in 1991.

For the second time in four days the elements were not very kind to England. The heavens opened shortly before the kick-off and most of the first half was played in heavy rain. England had made a handful of interesting

England's management team look on. Why were England not performing to the potential that they had shown during their 1995 Grand Slam?

changes which gave four players a golden opportunity to try to force their way into the senior side for the bigger matches ahead. With Will Carling nursing an injured ankle, Phil de Glanville was chosen at centre. Kyran Bracken, dropped after playing in all the 1995 Grand Slam matches, was given another chance at scrum-half. As Dean Richards was still recovering from his hamstring injury, Neil Back

was chosen at openside flanker to inject pace in the loose. Most interesting of all, there was a little cosmetic surgery in the front row. Victor Ubogu was dropped; Jason Leonard moved across to tight head, where he had played for the British Lions in the last two Tests against New Zealand in 1993, and Graham Rowntree was introduced at loose head.

That England could only equal Italy's try count in this match – each side scored two – says as much about Italy as it does about England. Afterwards, the England manager, Jack Rowell said, 'England lack the killer instinct at the moment and we are performing at a level a long way below our Five Nations form. I wish I knew the underlying reasons for this, but I can't come up with a satisfactory explanation. It is all very puzzling and worrying.'

Fortunately, just as in the opening game, England never looked like losing and they always had a comfortable cushion from the moment Tony Underwood gave them the lead in the eighth minute with an excellent try. Tim Rodber drove forward to set up an overlap deep in England's half. Rob Andrew seized the opportunity to

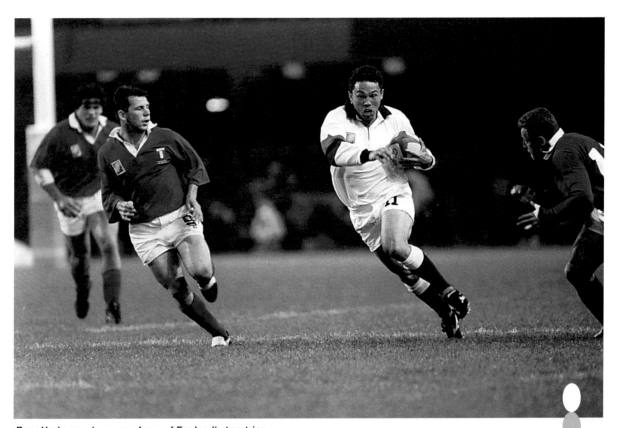

Rory Underwood, scorer of one of England's two tries against Italy, races through a gap in the Italian defence.

Massimo Cuttitta, the Italian captain, clears the ball to his fly-half, the former Puma Diego Dominguez.

open out and linked with the ever-alert Phil de Glanville to set free Mike Catt out on the right wing. He sprinted clear, drew the cover and released Tony Underwood to accelerate to the line to score an exhilarating and enterprising try. Andrew added the conversion and three penalties before half-time to put England in control. Diego Dominguez had managed one penalty midway through the half but at 16–3 it looked as if England would romp to a big win. However, in the 41st minute Mike Catt fielded an innocuous chip ahead near his own line which he should have cleared with ease. Surprisingly for a player whose cool head in his first full season for England has been much admired, he hesitated, and Paolo Vaccari not only charged down his kick but collected the ball on the bounce to score an opportunist try. It was 16–10, then, at half-time.

Early in the second half two touches of class from Rob Andrew and Mike Catt respectively put Rory Underwood over for his 43rd try for England. Andrew added two penalties for a very comfortable 27–10 lead going into the last quarter. At that point England, who had been going only at half-throttle anyway, took their foot off the accelerator altogether and allowed the Italians to claw their way back into the match. Ten minutes from the end Dominguez kicked a penalty and in the first minute of injury time he converted a try by his captain, Cuttitta, who, with a little help from his friends, had driven over the line from short range to take the final score to 27–20.

England had gained a place in the quarter-finals, but they had earned it in most unconvincing fashion. They were joined in the last eight by Western Samoa, who had also beaten Italy and Argentina but by playing much better rugby. A vociferous minority felt that the Western Samoans might well be good enough to beat England, especially when Jack Rowell decided to pick nine players who had not been first-choice selections in the Five Nations. There was even quite a lot of talk, would you believe, that the management had made a tactical decision to throw this match so they would be in the easier half of the draw come the quarter-final knock-out stages. The very idea of England deliberately trying to lose a rugby international is quite unthinkable, and it was

Brian Moore, Tim Rodber, Rob Andrew, Damian Hopley, Martin Bayfield and Ben Clarke enjoy the game against Western Samoa – the second-string side delivered England's most convincing performance yet.

amazing to see such a wide cross-section of usually informed opinion putting forward this theory.

The truth is much simpler and more straightforward. England had no strong preference about which side they faced in the quarter-finals. They acknowledged that it was going to be equally difficult to beat Australia at sea-level or South Africa at an altitude of 6,000ft in Johannesburg.

five and missed only one conversion, which was from the touchline.

That was in the opening minute of the match, during which the English forwards launched a major offensive and blasted huge holes in the normally tight Western Samoan defence. The pack, inspired by Victor Ubogu, drove to the line and Neil Back peeled off the maul to dive

Neil Back, England's flanker, confirms their early forward dominance with his first international try after only one and a half minutes of the crucial final pool match against Western Samoa.

What was important to them was to have all their key players available for selection in the knock-out stages, and consequently, they wisely rested several of their most important men. Rob Andrew, Jeremy Guscott and Tony Underwood were left out among the backs and up front Brian Moore, Jason Leonard, Martin Bayfield, Ben Clarke and Tim Rodber were given a game off. This most certainly did not mean that England were waving the white flag of surrender, as so many people suggested. They were taking sensible precautions to avoid risking injury to their key squad members against the very physical, abrasive and aggressive Western Samoans. England confounded their critics by producing their best rugby of the tournament thus far to win by the handsome score of 44–22. Jon Callard kicked five penalties out of

over in the corner. England had made it known that they meant business. The forwards were in rampant form and, despite the fact that most of the team had been plucked from the reserves, for the very first time in South Africa England looked like the champions of Europe. They produced a sparkling first 40 minutes as they raced to a 21–0 lead. Callard put over two penalties and converted a try by Rory Underwood which was created by powerful running in midfield by Ian Hunter. Mike Catt, who had unleashed the backs at every conceivable opportunity, put the seal on an excellent first-half performance with a neat dropped goal.

Having proved just how good they could be when they made the supreme effort, England seemed to have decided to hibernate for the first 20 minutes of the second half and allowed Western Samoa back into the match. No side is quicker to seize the initiative than these flamboyant warriors from the South Sea Islands. They threw everything at England with a bravura display of running rugby and they were rewarded with two tries in the space of five minutes, both scored by their replacement fly-half Fata Sini. On each occasion, after good lead-up work Sini darted through several half-hearted English tackles from 10 metres out to touch down near the posts.

Another penalty goal for each side left England ahead by only 24–17 midway through the half. But then Rip van Winkle awoke and they returned to their first-half dominance with a purple passage of play which produced 17 points in 12 minutes. The forwards earned a penalty try to confirm their superiority and Rory Underwood raced in for his third of the tournament after the forwards set up a driving ruck near halfway. Dewi Morris had made a sniping run down the blind side before linking with Dean

Richards, who gave his Leicester colleague the scoring pass. Callard added two conversions and two penalty goals for a lead of 44–17. The Western Samoans enjoyed the last word, if not much else, when their full-back, Mike Umaga, scored the seventh and final try of a highly entertaining game.

The message from Durban was clear – England were back on song, and they were quickly reinstated as one of the favourites for the World Cup. It was particularly encouraging that not only did established players such as Dewi Morris, Mike Catt, Rory Underwood and Jon Callard – who kicked superbly – all have exceptionally good games, but there were also some top-class performances from Phil de Glanville in the centre and new cap Richard West at lock. West settled into international rugby without the slightest difficulty. How the other Home Unions would love to have a player with his abundant promise.

Western Samoa, for their part, were also satisfied

Richard West, playing in his first international, makes a clean catch at a line-out. The form of the new-look England team was particularly encouraging for the rest of the squad.

England's Martin Bayfield wins some scrappy line-out ball ahead of Italy's Mark Giacheri and Pierpaolo Pedroni.

with the way Pool B had evolved. For the second World Cup in succession they had reached the quarter-finals, which is a tremendous achievement for a tiny country with a very small rugby-playing population. Their route to the top two in the pool looked straightforward after they overwhelmed Italy in their opening game. The final result, 42–18, told the whole story as the Western Samoan forwards had much the better of the set-piece exchanges, winning twice as much line-out ball. They were also quicker in the loose, where flanker Junior Paramore was outstanding. In the first half the Italians put up a very spirited resistance, trailing only 12–11 at the interval, but the continual pounding their forwards suffered eventually took its toll and the cracks appeared in the second half.

The Italian backs tackled pretty well, but the strong running and support play of the Samoans stretched their resources to the limit. The first try, in the tenth minute, was typical of the Western Samoans: they opened up from their own 22 to slip the Italian cover and allow their powerful wing, Brian Lima, to score. George Harder, an equally forthright runner, scored their second five minutes later, but Italy kept in touch with a try by Marcello Cuttitta and a dropped goal and penalty by fly-half Diego Dominguez. In the second half the Western Samoans played some very good rugby and were rewarded with another try apiece from Lima and Harder, plus two more from No. 8 Shem Tatupu and fly-half Darren Kellett respectively. Kellett added two conversions and two penalties. Italy had their one moment of glory midway through the half when Paolo Vaccari scored a try.

The Western Samoans were expected to have an

equally easy ride against Argentina, but they had reckoned without the phenomenal scrummaging of the Pumas. The Argentinians destroyed Western Samoa in this very important phase of play to such an extent that they had built up a lead of 26–13 by the middle of the second half. Their forwards scored two pushover tries: the first was actually a penalty try when the Samoans collapsed the scrum, and the second was touched down by scrum-half Rodrigo Crexell after the pack drove their opponents across the line. Fly-half José Cilley kicked one conversion and four penalty goals. However, in the last quarter of the match the Western Samoans staged a spectacular recovery and with two wonderful tries in the last five minutes and three penalty goals from Darren Kellett they

snatched a thrilling victory. Earlier on Kellett had converted two other penalties and a try by George Harder.

It was hard not to feel sorry for the Pumas, who had lost both their opening matches by just six points. Life got no better when they suffered precisely the same fate in their final match against Italy in which they were defeated by 31–25. It was another cracking game which the Pumas looked to have every chance of winning when they took a 25–24 lead ten minutes from the end. Their hopes were dashed by a late try by Italy's Diego Dominguez which rounded off a disastrous World Cup for Argentina. It had promised so much when they set off from Buenos Aires but ended with three defeats in three games, each by just

The Argentinian forwards show their power as they drive the England pack over their own line to get within six points of their opponents.

one score. Their problem is that their game is rather one-dimensional: they rely too much on their magnificent macho scrummaging. However, if they learn to use that as a means to an end and not as an end in itself, and if they develop their back play, they could once again become a major force on the international stage.

At half-time it was 12-12, but Italy's points came from four Dominguez penalties whereas Argentina got two tries through the power of their pack. Rolando Martin burst over after an initial surge from Féderico Mendez and the second was the customary penalty try. In the second half Italy hit back. Paolo Vaccari featured twice in a move which ended with him chipping over the cover defence and winning the race for the touchdown. Then came what

I believe was the best try of the World Cup.

From a scrum in midfield on the halfway line, the No. 8, Julian Gardner, picked up and drove across the gain-line. He passed inside to one flanker, Andrea Sgorlon, who slipped the ball on to the other, Orazio Arancio. He made 10 metres before passing to scrum-half Alessandro Troncon, who fed centre Stefano Bordon. Bordon handed on to Ivan Francescato, who side-stepped 25 metres to wrong-foot the defence. Lock forward Mark Giacheri was up in support and gave an overhead pass to Gardner. Under pressure, Gardner flipped the ball over his head without a moment's hesitation into the eager hands of Francescato, who flicked it on to Mario Gerosa. Gerosa completed the move with a fabulous try which deserved to win any match. In fact, it inspired the Pumas to one last effort which saw tries for Corral and Cilley and a penalty goal, also by Cilley, which regained the lead by one point. But then Dominguez scored his late try to give Italy victory.

So Argentina finished bottom of the pool, but at least they had the satisfaction of knowing that they were not far behind the top sides. Italy had two good matches out of three and had made considerable progress since the previous World Cup. Western Samoa confirmed their status among the top eight rugby-playing countries in the world, and if they manage to avoid losing their best players to either the New Zealand All Blacks or the lucrative lure of Rugby League, they will surely remain a major force. Despite their shaky start, England proved to be the best team in the pool and in the end they justified their position as the top seeded side. Their win over Western Samoa meant that they had to play Australia in the quarter-finals.

No sooner had England landed in Johannesburg than the world's top try-scorer and self-appointed leading critic of English rugby, the Wallaby winger David Campese, launched a withering attack on Will Carling and the whole England XV. Word of this stinging assault spread round South Africa in double-quick time. One inquisitive tabloid hack approached the England hooker, Brian Moore, to see if he had heard about Campese's invective. Moore said he had. The hack then asked: 'Is it fair to say that you hold David Campese in total and utter contempt?' Another journalist was heard to say, 'Methinks the prosecution is perhaps leading the witness, your honour.' But Moore refused to become involved in a slanging match. He replied that England would do all their talking on the pitch in Cape Town in the quarter-finals.

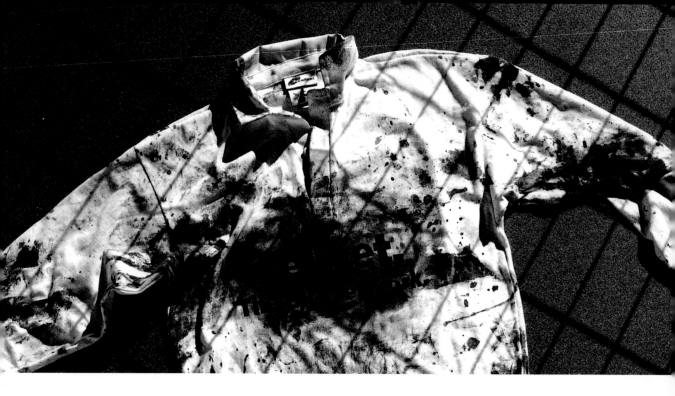

WE THOUGHT WE'D

BETTER TELL YOU

THAT THE NAME

ON THE SHIRT

IS 'CELLNET.'

Cellnet is an official supporter of the England 1995 Rugby World Cup Squad. In case you hadn't noticed.

THE NET THAT SETS YOU FREE.

Pool C
New Zealand - effective, efficient, overwhelming
Clem Thomas

After the stunning events of the opening match between South Africa and Australia and the attendant magnificence of the opening ceremony, culminating in the warm and emotional reception for Nelson Mandela, we knew that the events in this pool were going to be small beer indeed. It was obvious from the beginning that New Zealand were going to be in a class of their own and had nothing to beat, their opposition consisting of the two poorest teams, by some distance, in the Five Nations Championship, Ireland and Wales, together with the diminutive Japanese. It caused one South African journalist to remark, 'You ought to be ashamed of yourselves for playing against children.'

So impressive, effective, efficient and overwhelming were the All Blacks against such weak opponents that they were quickly promoted from second to first favourites to win the tournament, even though they had played no one of consequence in the pool matches. However, the pundits quickly recognised great quality in these All Blacks, for they always looked the most positive team in the competition. They had, however, lost a two-Test series to France at home during the previous English summer, and then won a three-Test series against South Africa, also at home, by a fairly narrow margin, taking the first two by 22–14 and 13–9 respectively, and drawing the final match 18–18. Before the tournament started, New Zealand were 100–30 against, both Wales and Ireland were 100–1 and Japan a hopeless 1,500–1. Inevitably, the bookmakers got it absolutely right. New Zealand cakewalked to the final, easily beating all the Four Home Unions on the way. The only real contest in this pool was between two equally poor teams, Ireland and Wales, who vied for the runners-up position and a place in the Durban quarter-final. There the successful team were to meet the first-placed side in Pool D, which, to the chagrin of the Scots (who, as runners-up faced the All Blacks in their quarter-final), and Gavin Hastings in particular, turned out to be France.

The Japanese were always going to be annihilated because of their size and, as Shiggy Konno, their spokesman for 40 years, plaintively said at the press conferences, 'I am always saying the same thing – we are simply not big enough.' For all that, Japan always played bravely and with extraordinary spirit, inventiveness and elan. Pound for pound they are as good as any team in the world, but because of their size they have suffered more than most from the new power game that rugby has become under laws which increasingly have legislated in favour of the big battalions to the exclusion of skill.

Never has this factor been better illustrated than in the emergence in this pool of such a freak player as the remarkable All Black Jonah Lomu, who, at 20 years old, quickly became the most feared individual in the World Cup. He was seen by his opponents, who must have had sleepless nights worrying about trying to stop him, as a cross between the Terminator and Frankenstein. As Brian Lochore, New Zealand's manager, said, tongue in cheek, 'We have had players as big as him before, but never on the wing.'

Before the pool games started, Wales travelled reluctantly with England and Argentina down to the inaugural lunch in Cape Town. On their return to Johannesburg via Durban, their aircraft struck an air pocket and plummeted a couple of hundred feet and they were scared to death. One of the first to recover his equilibrium and his voice was Alex Evans, Wales' coach, who was heard to say in his Aussie twang, 'I don't mind going down with these English bastards, but I am worried about getting eaten by these Argies.' As it turned out, they were eaten by everybody else in their pool apart from the Japanese.

Wales showed once more that they are a country in disarray, which is, perhaps, not altogether surprising considering that most of their best players in recent years have defected to Rugby League. No country in the world could sustain such losses and credibly challenge for the World Cup. Imagine what the presence of such players as Jonathan Davies, arguably one of the great fly-halves of our time, David Young, Paul Moriarty, Scott Quinnell, Alan Bateman, Scott Gibbs and John Devereux would do for Wales now. The English argument that they are as badly affected is simply not true, for Rugby League just

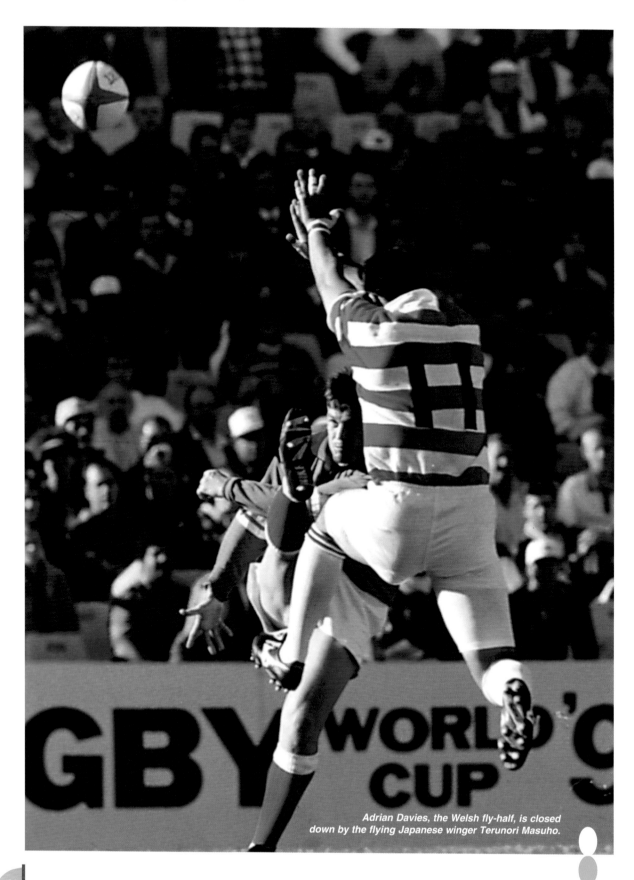

Adrian Davies, the Welsh fly-half, is closed down by the flying Japanese winger Terunori Masuho.

does not seem to take the established players whom they have nurtured. Wales were the first of the eight major International Board countries to suffer the indignity of having to qualify for this World Cup, having to beat Romania, Portugal, Spain and Italy to qualify as the team from Europe 1. Then came a disastrous winter in which they lost at home to South Africa by 22–10 and were then whitewashed in the Five Nations tournament. There followed the usual self-destructive ploy of sacking their coaches, Alan Davies and Gareth Jenkins, and their manager, Bob Norster; then, far too late in the day, introducing Cardiff's Australian, Alex Evans, as chief coach with Mike Ruddock and Dennis John as assistants and Geoff Evans as manager. Changing horses in midstream was inviting calamity, and so it proved. We saw badly selected teams with little idea of what to do, poor morale and scant appetite for battle.

The Irish were not expected to do well either, for they had lost heavily to England, Scotland and France in the Five Nations Championship, saving themselves from the ignominy of the wooden spoon only by beating Wales in Cardiff. Furthermore, they had lost disastrously to Italy in May by 22–10. Japan had shocked everybody with a win over Romania by 34–21, but two losses to Tonga also suggested that the World Cup seedings might not be as good as they ought to be. Surely sides like Fiji and the USA would have been better bets, and of far higher quality, than the Ivory Coast or Japan?

The first match in Pool C was between Japan and Wales at Bloemfontein, in the superb new Free State Stadium. It must be said that South Africa is the land of great rugby stadia, and nowhere in the world can compare in this respect.

The match itself re-emphasised the difference between Caucasian and Oriental physique and, like the other games in which Japan were involved, perhaps showed the futility of their cause. It is a sad but realistic judgement that the Japanese are simply not big enough to compete at this level. They lack nothing else but size, but although they are the strictest keepers of the faith, in terms of the real spirit of rugby, and are colourful, brave, never give up and play with more flair and enthusiasm than most, they remain a pushover, even for the poorer established teams such as Ireland or Wales.

The comparative ease of the Welsh win made it difficult to tell whether their new coaching team had cooked up a different recipe from the same old ingredients, players whose morale remained pretty low

after their recent losses. At one training session, the coach, trying hard to put some steel into the side, was heard to say, 'That was a bit bloody sedate, wasn't it?' There were some interesting changes in the Welsh team, particularly the ploy of playing Adrian Davies at fly-half and putting Neil Jenkins at inside centre, and bringing in the new Bridgend centre, Gareth Thomas, on the wing. It all seemed to work pretty well, as Wales got a good result in spite of obviously relaxing and losing concentration in the second half. Both Andy Moore, deputising at scrum-half for the rested Robert Jones, and Gareth Thomas scored tries on their debuts. Thomas's three tries were a record for a Welsh debut and earned him rave notices from the coach, who said that he was exactly the sort of player Wales were looking for.

From the start, the Welsh forwards gave Japan the inevitable problem of holding their forward drives as they imposed all the early pressure. It brought them three penalty goals from Jenkins in the first 20 minutes – one of them a huge kick from way out on the halfway line, which was an early illustration of how far the ball could travel in the rarified atmosphere of the high veld. Having gained a comfortable lead, Wales cut loose for the only time in the tournament. Andy Moore and Ieuan Evans scored well-taken tries, both converted by Jenkins, who also added another penalty. Further tries by Ieuan Evans and Gareth Thomas brought them a handsome 36–0 advantage at half-time.

Soon after the interval Gareth Thomas touched down his second try, converted by Jenkins for 43–0, but thereafter Wales rested on their laurels and, instead of pressing home their advantage à la All Blacks, they earned criticism for not continuing their attack. Midway through the half, the brave Japanese created wave after wave of pressure and were rewarded with a well-deserved try by Lopeti-Tuimo Oto. The Japanese, scampering around the field, were now seriously embarrassing the Welsh defence, but finally Wales renewed their attack and tries by Gareth Thomas and Hemi Taylor, both converted by Jenkins, resulted in a comfortable win, even though Japan had the last word with another try by Oto. Japan had played their hearts out, but to no avail. Their best players were their three Tongans, the two unrelated Latus in the back row and Oto on the right wing.

Next came our first interesting glimpse of New Zealand who, at this stage, were only third favourites to win the Cup, as they took on the Irish at Ellis Park. And it was a far better contest than the 43–19 result might

The towering Ian Jones, one of the forwards of the tournament, wins a line-out against Ireland's Gabriel Fulcher.

The shape of things to come. Jonah Lomu leaves a trail of destruction in his wake as he scores the first of his tries against Ireland.

suggest – the score, like so many others were to be, was distorted by the extraordinary Lomu, who, in this his first game of the tournament, exploded on to the scene like a giant genie. In his opening match he became a one-man army, and had every coach in the World Cup reaching for the valium and wondering how on earth his players were going to stop him. In fact Ireland played their best rugby in South Africa in this game. From the word go they gave it a mighty crack, unleashing a barrage of garryowens to disconcert the All Blacks and generally giving them a pretty torrid time. The Irish deservedly drew first blood, driving Halpin over for a try converted by Eric Elwood. Unfortunately, Elwood's kicking skills then deserted him for the rest of the game.

The new All Black outside-half, Andrew Mehrtens, who had shown that he was more than adequately filling the huge hole left by the departure of Grant Fox, already looks a truly great player in the making. Despite his two penalty goals Ireland still led after half an hour. Inevitably, it was Lomu who did the damage. He took off on one of his unstoppable runs to set up a try for Walter Little, who consistently looked the best centre in the tournament. Mehrtens converted and then Frank Bunce charged down a kick for a try, again converted by Mehrtens, and suddenly the All Blacks were in charge.

Then came a wonderful Irish try. It began 70 yards out with a drive by Popplewell; a pass by Elwood was brilliantly picked up by Simon Geoghegan from his shoelaces and the flying Irish winger made a tremendous break and a marvellous long run before passing inside to the supporting Jonathan Bell. He was tackled near the line, but the ever-eager Denis McBride was on hand to pick up and score. Yet thereafter the amazing Lomu ran away with the game. He scored a try and Mehrtens kicked a penalty. It was Lomu who, again, had the crowd whooping with glee with another fearsome run, which saw him break tackle after tackle. In the end it was the smallest Irishman, Geoghegan, who got him around ankle-height. It was not enough to prevent that other New Zealand dynamo, Josh Kronfeld, from scoring.

Ireland, in their determination to come to grips with the game, conceded far too many penalties and another Mehrtens kick took the All Blacks out of reach. To their credit, the Irish never gave up. A try by the ever-busy David Corkery, which Elwood did manage to convert, made the gap respectable until a final try by Glen Osborne for New Zealand clearly showed who were the masters.

Ireland's spirited performance is rewarded with a try for David Corkery.

power began to tell. They were awarded a second penalty try for a collapsed scrum, which, together with a close-quarter try by Eddie Halvey and two conversions from Burke, put them comfortably in the lead once again. Still the Japanese kept coming, and a try by their captain and hooker, Masahiro Kunda, converted by Yoshida, kept Ireland on their toes before another penalty goal by Burke and a try by Niall Hogan, also converted by Burke, sealed the match at 50–28.

Welsh lock forward Greg Prosser wins some comfortable line-out ball against New Zealand.

As the All Black captain, Sean Fitzpatrick, said afterwards, 'The Irish, as ever, played like madmen for the first 30 minutes, but once we got control we were home and dry.' Terry Kingston, the Irish skipper, who seemed fairly cheerful about his team's performance, commented, 'We gave it an almighty lash, but we made too many basic errors.'

Ireland were the next to put Japan on the chopping block, but it was less of a walkover than had been expected. Japan courageously scored four tries to Ireland's seven – and two of the Irish scores were penalty tries for collapsed scrums on the line, and were thus entirely due to superior weight. Indeed, Ireland had to depend heavily on the strength of their pack, for the Japanese were all over them in the loose. Nevertheless, they won comfortably in the end and set up the big shoot-out with Wales for a place in the quarter-finals.

The Irish began well enough – they were 19 points up after 20 minutes with tries by David Corkery, Neil Francis and Simon Geoghegan, and two conversions by Paul Burke, who was giving Eric Elwood a rest. The Japanese then retaliated with two very good tries of their own from Sinali Latu and Ko Izawa, a temporary replacement for Sione Latu. Yoshida converted both to make it 19–14 at half-time. Things remained hairy in the second half for, although Ireland quickly increased their lead to 26–14 with a pushover try two minutes after the interval, the Japanese continued to run rings around them in the loose and were far quicker to the loose ball. Midway through the half, Hirao scored a lovely try and Japan were still in the game and looking ominous. It was pull-yourself-together time for the Irish, and finally their forward

New Zealand versus Wales was seen as a formality, considering that Wales had not beaten the All Blacks since 1953, when the Test record between the two countries stood at 3–1 in Wales' favour. It is now 13–3 to New Zealand. In their current plight, there was nothing at all to suggest that the Welsh had a prayer. To make matters worse, the selectors chose a strange side, selecting Gareth Llewellyn, a lock with no pretensions to speed, on

Walter Little's path is blocked by Greg Prosser. The All Black centre had an outstanding tournament.

the flank of the scrum. New Zealand, on the other hand, took no chances and selected their best available team. Surprisingly, in view of their other results, they managed to beat Wales only by the modest score of two goals, one try, four penalty goals and a dropped goal to two penalties and a dropped goal.

In this game, the All Blacks' outstanding player was South African-born Andrew Mehrtens, who played with an authority and an assurance far beyond his 22 years. Wales failed to cross the New Zealand line but they battled hard – indeed, they even managed to draw first blood with a dropped goal by Neil Jenkins after five minutes. New Zealand's response was quick. They began to win the loose ball with ominous ease, and continued to do so in a ratio 2:1 for the rest of the match, which was not surprising when Wales were playing three slow second-row forwards. As the pressure told, Mehrtens soon kicked a penalty. The All Blacks used him to kick for territory, and then unleashed their backs. Ominously, they were too easily breaking the gain-line. After 18 minutes the Welsh defence was pierced by that fine centre Walter Little. Mehrtens converted and then kicked another penalty. Four minutes from half-time, a sweetly won ruck saw the All Blacks spread the ball wide to Marc Ellis, who scored for Mehrtens to convert. At the end of the first half, New Zealand led comfortably by 20–3.

Jenkins kicked a penalty goal for Wales soon after the interval, but Mehrtens replied with two for New Zealand. Another penalty for Jenkins was by now irrelevant: the All Blacks were almost entirely in control of the rucks and the loose ball, where Wales were pitifully slow to the breakdown. The Welsh then put in their best passage of play in the tournament, making a series of running attacks which, for a while, had New Zealand reeling in the corner. Their only reward was a penalty, which Jenkins missed. The All Blacks came back with a vengeance and a dropped goal by Mehrtens, and another storming run by the almost unstoppable Lomu, brought a try for Josh Kronfeld, who had a marvellous World Cup. This finished off Wales who, nevertheless, conceded fewer points to the eventual finalists than any other side.

So once again Wales had lost to the excellence of New Zealand, but they had contributed to their own defeat by choosing a back row which was unequal to the task, and they paid the penalty. Coach Alex Evans told the media that he believed it was the pace at which the game was played in the southern hemisphere that made the northern hemisphere teams look so disjointed. The wet

Marc Ellis, the All Black who scored a record six tries during the 145-17 massacre of Japan.

weather in the northern hemisphere makes the game slower, a fact which gives even more credence to Gavin Hastings' demand in his recent book for the Five Nations to be played in the summer months.

The penultimate game in Pool C was to see records fall like confetti as New Zealand proceeded to demolish poor Japan by the record score of 145-17. It was, of course, total destruction, and it again underlined the complete futility of small people competing in the new heavyweight game that rugby has become. The All Blacks were in one of their unkind moods and one felt that, if they had been playing their grandmothers at croquet that day, then they would have smashed them off the court. One of the more astonishing performances was the place-kicking of Simon Culhane, who converted 20 of the 21 New Zealand tries, one of which he scored himself, to break by one point Gavin Hastings' individual world

record of 44 set earlier in the competition against the Ivory Coast in Pool D.

All the World Cup records tumbled – the most points, most tries and most conversions. The try-scorers for New Zealand were: Marc Ellis (6), Jeff Wilson (3), Eric Rush (3), Robin Brooke (2), Glen Osborne (2), and Richard Loe, Craig Dowd, Paul Henderson, Simon Culhane and Alama Ieremia (1 apiece). For Japan, Keiji Hirose kicked a penalty, and the eager Hiroyuki Kajihara got two brave second-half tries, which Hirose converted. So the All Blacks duly topped the pool and prepared for their quarter-final against Scotland.

The last, and perhaps the most unpredictable game of the pool was the key match between those Celtic cousins Ireland and Wales for a place in the quarter-finals against the French. Nobody expected much in the way of quality rugby and they did not get it. Both teams played a game

The Irish support was as colourful as ever before the all-important clash with Wales.

which qualified, together with the France–England play-off match, as the worst in the tournament. For the second time running Wales failed to pass the pool stage and went home to a once proud rugby nation in disgrace. Many of their players voiced the view that they were afraid to go home until the furore over their poor performance subsided, and indeed many of them did stay on in South

Africa for the heat to die down.

The sheer ineptitude of both sides in this match would be hard to beat. Wales even gave Ireland a 14-point start and gifted them two tries from set pieces in the first 11 minutes. The first came from a disciplined drive from a line-out won by Gabriel Fulcher. Nick Popplewell wrestled his way over and Eric Elwood converted. The

*Gabriel Fulcher gains possession for Ireland against Wales
in the shambolic battle for a quarter-final place.*

second was even more absurd. Denis McBride, the smallest chap at the end of the line, grabbed a long ball and fell to the ground. The Welshmen stood there and gaped as he got up and raced through to score what was the softest try of the tournament. From hereon in, Wales played catch-up rugby, and not very successfully at that: their midfield play was simply atrocious and their ball retention was almost non-existent. Therefore they were totally unable to gain any control, particularly as Ireland's rucking and mauling were more disciplined and assertive. Even so, the Irish were equally devoid of ideas in the backs and their principal means of attack was the old up-and-under, which, though it wasn't until late in the game, allowed Wales some opportunity for counter-attack.

Wales slowly clawed their way back into contention by means of the boot of Neil Jenkins, who kicked a penalty goal and a dropped goal in the first half. When he put over another penalty 14 minutes into the second period, Wales' fightback seemed to be gaining ground. They were foiled when, ten minutes before the end, Eddie Halvey, who came on as a blood replacement for McBride, powered his way over for a try which was converted by Elwood. With only about seven minutes to go, Wales, playing with urgency for the first time, managed a try themselves. A long pass by Robert Jones, by far the best Welsh player throughout, found his club-mate Tony Clement, who forced his way through to put hooker John Humphreys over the line. Jenkins converted, and it was only 21–16 to Ireland with six minutes left. A late penalty by Elwood clinched their victory, even though in injury time Wales scored a final try through Hemi Taylor which again was converted by

Simon Geoghegan, Ireland's wing threequarter, was one of the few players to shine in one of the most disappointing games of the tournament.

Jenkins, to bring them to within one point of Ireland at 24–23.

It was the sort of game which neither side deserved to win, for it appeared that you could not pick a decent side from both teams. Yet even the Welsh conceded that Ireland had played with more passion and determination and therefore deserved to go through. There was, however, a great gnashing of teeth in Wales over the matter and the chairman of the Welsh Rugby Union,

Vernon Pugh, who was in South Africa, threatened to resign unless comprehensive changes were made to the structure and coaching of the game in Wales. We may, then, see some action in the Principality next year, and not before time. They could start by ensuring that they do not lose any more players to the professional game, wherein lies the Welsh Achilles' heel. For their part, Ireland were well content to get to the quarters, which always was their realistic target.

Ireland's players share their relief with the crowd. Victory meant a quarter-final against France. For Wales, it was the early flight home for the second successive tournament.

IT TAKES SKILL, DEDICATION AND TEAMWORK TO GET TO THE TOP.

Best wishes from one great team to the others.

Pool D
Scots breached by French miracle move
Bill McLaren

Scotland presented themselves for the opening salvos of the 1995 World Cup in very good heart and with justifiable ambition to reach the knock-out stages and then to take it from there. Their squad had a rich leavening of foot soldiers of long service, such as the Hastings brothers, Craig Chalmers, Tony Stanger, Ken Milne, Paul Burnell and Damian Cronin, in a mix with comparative newcomers who had made their mark in the Five Nations Championship and for whom the World Cup was to prove a memorable experience. Among those were Craig Joiner, Kenny Logan, Bryan Redpath, Derrick Patterson, David Hilton, Kevin McKenzie, Stewart Campbell, Peter Walton, Rob Wainwright and Eric Peters.

This, after all, was the squad which had created a resurgence in Scottish fortunes which had lifted the entire nation. They consigned that dismal record of nine consecutive games without a win to the history books with a run of four victories in a row over Canada (22–6), Ireland (26–13), France (23–21) and Wales (26–13). True, they then lost a Grand Slam decider to England at Twickenham by 24–12, a match that, sadly, spawned not a single try, but history had been made when Gavin Hastings, with a singular tour de force, led his side to victory in Paris for the first time in 26 years. The Scots then proceeded to put Romania to the sword by 49–16 at Murrayfield prior to departing for a week at altitude in Spain which culminated in a 62–7 (ten tries to one) defeat of the Spanish national side in a no-caps game in Madrid.

Rustenburg provided the splendid backdrop for the final match of Pool D – Tonga against the Ivory Coast. The game, however, was marred by the tragic injury to Max Brito.

So Scotland's World Cup preparations had gone well. They had been meticulously arranged to give the squad maximum exposure to the hazards of playing and training at altitude. Early arrival in Pretoria, which was to be their base for their pool games, also underlined the resolve to give Scotland every opportunity to reach peak performance when the starter's gun sounded.

Pool D didn't look all that hazardous. The Ivory Coast (or the Côte d'Ivoire, as they insisted on being called) were newcomers to the international fold, having played their first international in 1990; Tonga had been beaten 23–5 by a Scottish team containing only Kenny Logan, Ian Jardine, Ian Smith and Doddie Weir of the World Cup squad during Scotland's 1993 tour of the South Pacific. That victory gave confidence that the full Scottish side could see off the Tongans. France presented the most formidable hurdle to Scottish aspirations to winning the pool. First and second placings in Pool D were significant because the winners seemed certain to meet Ireland or Wales in the quarter-finals while the runners-up appeared destined to take on New Zealand. There seemed to be a general consensus that Wales or Ireland would be a more inviting prospect than the formidable All Blacks, who could be expected to emerge from an uncharacteristically unsuccessful period with renewed vigour, commitment and ambition.

Each pool match carried three points for a win, two for a draw, one for a loss and none for any team deciding not to play or abandoning a match. It was encouraging that in the event of a drawn game, the team scoring most tries had the better chance of taking three points for a win. It was an amusing condition that, all else having failed to decide the tie, the winner would be the side having the least number of players ordered off or, finally, the team winning the toss of a coin.

No such measures were required to decide Scotland's opening pool game against the Ivory Coast, which was to give immense pleasure to the rugby folk of Rustenburg, a rural community some 50 kilometres from Pretoria on the way to Sun City. This was to be the first Rugby Union

Kevin McKenzie, the Scottish No. 2, emulates the dive pass of a scrum-half. During Scotland's game against the Ivory Coast it seemed that anything was possible.

Gavin Hastings touches down to score one of his four tries in an overall world-record points tally of 44 points. The record was to last for just nine days, after which New Zealand's Simon Culhane eclipsed it by a single point.

international to be staged in the Olympia Park Stadium there, and the locals, mostly from the farming community or platinum miners, went out of their way to bid a warm welcome to their visitors. They had even bought a huge stand from the Loftus Versveld Stadium in Pretoria. It made a wonderful sight as thousands of supporters basked in the evening sunshine while taking in a match of flowing action and 13 tries.

Scotland's selectors faced something of a dilemma over the choice of personnel for the Ivory Coast game. They would have preferred to have played Tonga first with their strongest side, then given some of the key men a break from the Ivory Coast match in preparation for the crucial game against France. Instead there was the problem of whether to play the heavy artillery in all three games or to open against the Africans with a team below recognised maximum strength and experience. In the event they decided to take no chances. Scotland wanted to get off to a cracking start so they fielded virtually the XV which had beaten the Romanians handsomely just a month previously. It was of some concern that as David

Hilton was nursing an ankle injury Paul Burnell was drafted in to play at loose head in an international for only the second time. It was encouraging, though, that the big Northampton loose forward Peter Walton was back in harness and that Kevin McKenzie's challenge to Ken Milne for the hooker's spot was acknowledged in his selection for the first match although, in typically dogged fashion, Milne restated his credentials by being first choice for the following three games. There was speculation that Tony Stanger and Graham Shiel might be installed as the number one centre pairing after their handsome contributions to the defeat of Romania, but, to his credit, Scott Hastings achieved such a level of sharpness and commitment in training that he forced himself back as number one outside centre for the other games.

The Scots knew a little about the Ivory Coast, but not a lot. They knew they had been training at altitude near Poitiers in France during April; that they had beaten the French clubs Angoulême (29–15) and La Teste (23–7); that they were very heavy up front; that they had a large, well-nourished soul on the left wing called Celestin

The Scots run riot. No. 6 Peter Walton charges through the Ivory Coast's midfield, supported by Rob Wainwright and Kevin McKenzie.

N'Gbala who could be troublesome in space, and that some observers had likened them to the Fijians in their willingness to run the ball from unexpected situations. The Ivory Coast were so keen to do well. They had beaten Namibia and Zimbabwe in the qualifying stages and for everyone in their likeable squad this induction to life in the fast lane of World Cup rugby was a mind-boggling undertaking, the experience of a lifetime. There was, too, a citizen with the build of a hay barn and what looked like a 30in neck, called Toussaint Djehi. He was a 17½st tight-head prop who, apparently, had dished out a bit of yahoo in a singularly ill-tempered game against Namibia. Yet, off the pitch, Djehi was the life and soul of the party, a happy-go-lucky, friendly fellow who, as it turned out, didn't give Paul Burnell any trouble at all.

Although 11 of the Ivorians play their club rugby in France, they just didn't get a look-in against Scotland, who won the line-outs 23–10, ran tap-offence kicks nine times and scored their 13 tries in a riot of running and passing which had all the appearance of a sevens game. The Scottish domination of possession can be gauged from the statistics which show that Bryan Redpath received the ball 59 times to Frederic Dupont's 18 and that Craig Chalmers passed the ball 31 times while his rival, Athanase Dali, had only five passes. Dali was a key figure in the Ivory Coast side and was unlucky to be stretchered off after 25 minutes, by which time Scotland were 13–0 ahead and like greyhounds in the slips. They went on to win by 89–0.

There was, too, another monumental display from Gavin Hastings. He opened Scotland's account with the first of his four tries and closed it by converting, with unfailing accuracy, the last try, dotted down by Ken Logan. Hastings Senior set a new world record of 44 points in an international with four tries, nine conversions and two penalty goals. True, it didn't last for long – only until Simon Culhane of New Zealand registered 45 points against Japan. But Culhane scored just one try and 20 conversions, whereas Hastings was in on everything against the Ivorians. Scotland's other try-scorers were Stanger, Shiel, Logan (two), Chalmers, Burnell, Peter Wright and Ian Morrison (two). The Scottish 89-point margin of victory also stood as a world record until New Zealand later beat Japan by 145–17. Of course, Hong Kong had defeated Singapore by 164–13 and Ashley Billington scored ten tries for 50 points in the same match, but that was in a World Cup qualifier and not in the final stages.

Scotland were expecting a hard time from the Tongans. They knew that the Pacific Islanders were renowned for their ferocious, unorthodox style of tackling in which making 'big hits' was the aim. They knew, too, that the King of Tonga, himself a former lock forward at Sydney University, had not been amused by the Tongans' 75–5 defeat by Canterbury in the Super-10 series. King Taufa Ahau Tupou IV did a bit of plain speaking to the World Cup squad. I'm sure His Majesty wouldn't use such

from the tournament. There was much talk about whether Mahoni was in fact the guilty party, but the Tongan management did not use the appeal procedure and Mahoni went home.

That sad episode seemed only to heighten Tongan resolve in their match with Scotland. They had a tight five averaging 16st 8lbs, two Vunipola brothers, Manu and Elisi, at half-back and a third, Fe'ao, at hooker, and a 16st right wing called Alaska Taufa who could prove a handful. Tonga earned a lot of criticism for the nature of some of their tackling and their offside play, although there was

The Tongans tackled ferociously throughout the tournament. Here the French centre, Thierry Lacroix, appears rather eager to offload the ball.

rich language as 'get your fingers out or else', but whatever his words were, they seemed sure to act as an incentive to these proud islanders, descended from great warriors of the past. One unexpected factor that it was thought might influence the Tongan approach to the Scottish game was a natural resentment that their lock forward Feleti Mahoni had been sent off in the French match by England referee Steve Lander and dismissed

slick handling and intuitive running of the ball in the creation of their opening try, scored by a splendid flank forward, Ipolito Fenukitau. By that stage, Scotland already had three penalty goals from Gavin Hastings, but the Tongan try cut the deficit to 9–5 and sounded the alarm bells in Scottish ranks. It was, however, a clear indication of Tongan indiscipline that Gavin Hastings was allowed to equal the world record of eight penalty goals in an

Aubin Hueber leads the French counter-attack against Tonga, supported well by Marc Cecillon.

international, held by Mark Wyatt (Canada), Neil Jenkins (Wales) and Diego Dominguez (Italy) and later matched by Thierry Lacroix (France). As the Scottish captain also scored a try and conversion for 31 points, he stood at the top of the World Cup scorers with 75 points in just two games.

Yet the Scots, in a sense, went into their shells during this game. At the same time, they were not able to open the ball wide because of Tonga's craft in preventing fair release at breakdown points. Craig Chalmers used the boot to turn the islanders and Ian Jardine, who had been introduced at centre along with Scott Hastings, barely allowed the ball to go beyond him but was content to cut back to the haven of the pack. There was also a clear desire on the part of the Scots to avoid setting up colleagues for some of those big hits with which the Tongans tend to intimidate their opponents. The plan worked, although it was not all that pretty. The Scots

were given 71 per cent of the offence rucks; Tonga only 29. Craig Chalmers had the ball 23 times to Elisi Vunipola's ten. Scotland also won the line-outs 20–11, Doddie Weir enhancing his reputation as Scotland's number one supplier. The full-strength Scottish pack – Hilton, Milne, Wright, Cronin, Weir, Wainwright, Peters, Morrison – were beginning to work up a fair head of steam which was to stand them in good stead for later challenges. Scotland's other tries were by the flying Scott Hastings and Eric Peters, who was proving an integral part of a well-balanced breakaway unit. So the Tongans were seen off by 41–5, and with 130 points and 16 tries in the pouch, the Scots were virtually certain to qualify for the knock-out stages.

Perhaps the most difficult selectorial decision Scotland faced concerned the centre berths. Shiel had been in magnificent form against the Ivory Coast. His sprint training during the summer had given him an extra yard

Yann Delaigue, the French fly-half, stops the Tongan charge with some solid tackling.

and this seemed to have lifted his confidence so that now he was looking for opportunities for incisive running to set alongside his other skilled accomplishments. There was the feeling that his edge of pace was essential in midfield, and so it proved – he was selected for both the France and New Zealand internationals.

Meanwhile, the French had been keeping a fairly low profile, or as low as possible considering the vast numbers of their media people who thronged their hotel and training areas in search of scoop material. In beating Tonga 38–10 in Pretoria they set no heather on fire, their forwards gaining little advantage in scrummage or line-out; their backs finding it hard to stitch together those rippling movements for which they are famed. It took a dropped goal by Yann Delaigue and three penalty goals by Thierry Lacroix to give them a cushion and the confidence to spin the ball. The match marked a triumph for Lacroix, who registered 25 points with two tries, three penalty

goals and three conversions. The other French tries came from their captain, Philippe Saint-André, his 21st, and scrum-half Aubin Hueber. France were comfortably in command at 38–3 before conceding a late try to Tevita Va'enuku.

One curious development in the French camp was the decision of their backs, with the exception of Christophe Deylaud, to shave their heads. Such a gesture, which served only to give them the appearance of moving billiard balls, was hard to understand. Some attributed this collective eccentricity to a desire to make an all-for-one-and-one-for-all policy of unity in their cause; others held that it was the backs' method of expressing some displeasure with their coach, Pierre Berbizier. Many thought the African sun had got to them. In any event, they were all as bald as coots, even such a sensible veteran as Philippe Sella. It created something of a nightmare for commentators, and especially for the more aged among them, in trying to identify which bald head belonged to whom. One recalls that occasion some seasons ago when the Racing Club de France won the French club championship final despite playing throughout in stiff, starched collars and bow-ties. Franck Mesnel was among that band; he was also in the World Cup squad. Any connection? Who knows?

Anyway, the French sailed through by 54–18 against the Ivory Coast. Their halves, Delaigue and Guy Accoceberry, received a constant supply of later-phase ball and Lacroix had another field day with 20 points from two tries, two conversions and two penalty goals. The other tries came from Accoceberry, Abdel Benazzi and Arnaud Costes and Deylaud kicked two conversions.

So, as expected, Pool D resolved itself into a Scotland–France shoot-out for the privilege of dodging the All Blacks in the semi-final. French coach Berbizier was philosophical about the outcome, claiming that

Rob Wainwright, tracked closely by Guy Accoceberry, pounces on the loose ball during the crucial clash in Pool D. The losers of the game would have to face the might of the All Blacks.

whereas Ireland or Wales might be slightly easier opposition, anyone seeking to win the World Cup simply had to beat everyone else, and if it came down to France versus New Zealand, so be it. Despite the shaven heads and French failure to put it all together in the first two pool games, Berbizier kept his sense of humour. When I asked him if he regarded Gavin Hastings as the big danger to French aspirations he asked, 'Gavin who?'

'Andrew Gavin Hastings,' I elucidated.

'Oh, that Gavin Hastings,' he said with a huge smile.

Berbizier, as the New Zealand coach, Laurie Mains, was to do later, expressed high admiration for Scotland's captain and for his behaviour on and off the field.

It was a great match, arguably the best of the tournament, and at the end almost everyone in the Loftus Versfeld Stadium was hoarse following one of the most dramatic ever finishes to an international match. Scotland, their pack matching the opposition's in every phase, led 13–3 at half-time through two penalty goals by Gavin Hastings and his conversion of a magnificent try by Rob Wainwright, which owed much to the quick wits and reactive skill of Bryan Redpath and a thundering charge by Scotland's captain up the left touchline. There was a feeling among the cognoscenti that Hastings would win the game with his goal-kicking as Thierry Lacroix was not reliable, too much of a hot-and-cold kicker. In the event, Lacroix kept France in the hunt with five penalty goals out of five attempts. He was, unfortunately, for Scotland, very hot in this match! Yet Hastings, who also had five successful kicks at goal, kept Scottish noses in front at 16–9 and 19–15 and, on the trend of play, no one could have begrudged Scotland a victory for their manner in taking the game to the French, not flamboyantly, but with clinical, percentage rugby, superbly brave tackling, especially round the fringes, and clear intent, expressed early in the game by Hastings Senior, that they were going to attack the French, ball in hand, at every reasonable opportunity. They did so in thrilling style, while throughout France held the threat of startling riposte from the deep that produced, in 1991 at Twickenham and 1994 in Auckland, the long-range tries of stunning creativity that have set the French apart as the most lethal counter-attackers in the world.

Scotland's moment of heartbreak arrived with only 20

Olivier Roumat gets a helping hand from his team-mates.

seconds of actual playing time remaining. Indeed, referee Wayne Erickson of Australia had already taken one more look at his watch and had probably made up his mind to blow for no-side as soon as the ball next became dead. As Scotland clung to their 19–15 lead, France launched a last despairing attack. Two forward thrusts, one by Benazzi, who was one of the forwards of the tournament, dislocated Scotland's defence alignment, whereupon Deylaud's rifled pass missed both centres and was gathered in by Emile Ntamack, who had materialised like

a quarter-final in Pretoria against the All Blacks, who had amassed 29 tries and conceded just five in their three pool games. All the same, Scotland had every reason for pride in their performances. They had set the pool competition alight with some gorgeous running rugby against the Ivory Coast; they had kept their heads and their discipline despite provocation in the Tonga game, and they had deserved to win against France. Nevertheless, they paid tribute to the fighting qualities of the French side, who, despite trailing virtually throughout, had kept their cool

The crucial moment. Emile Ntamack powers his way past Scott Hastings to score the last-minute winning try for the French.

an animated prairie dog on the left flank with his captain, Saint-André, outside him. Scott Hastings on the drift made a valiant effort to sink Ntamack short of the line, but at 6ft 2in and weighing almost 14^1/$_2$ st, the French wing was unstoppable. To add insult to injury, Lacroix slotted the touchline conversion with consummate ease. France were through by 22–19 in the most captivating fashion, and with a winning try out of the French book of miracle moves.

It was a shattering blow to the Scots. They now faced

and had prevailed in typically Gallic style.

There was some criticism of the Scottish selection panel because Cameron Glasgow, John Manson and Jeremy Richardson were not given a game. Perhaps if the Ivory Coast match had been Scotland's second those three would have been chosen. It must be thoroughly frustrating for players to give their all at every training session, to reach a peak of fitness not previously experienced, to be raring to take the field, and yet to be obliged to spend a month in a foreign land without actually playing in the World Cup. At least Manson and Richardson have their names in the records as capped players. Glasgow hasn't, and that first game against the Africans would have been an ideal vehicle for his particular gifts of deceptive running, change of pace and general level of skill. He is such a versatile player as to be of immense value on the bench, and it should not be too long before he joins his father, Ron, capped ten times as a flanker in the 1960s, in the ranks of international players.

One of the unusual features of Scotland's World Cup which sent a wave of sadness and concern throughout the rugby world as well as redoubling the desire to take every possible precaution to ensure that players do not come to serious physical harm on the rugby field. The match was barely five minutes old when Max Brito, the Ivorian left wing, suffered a serious injury which left him paralysed for life. Such misery not only evokes massive sympathy for his wife and family but also makes one ponder whether emergent rugby nations still 'learning the trade', as it were, should be pitted against far more experienced

The face of despair. Gavin Hastings contemplates defeat at the hands of the French. He later admitted that it was a game his side had the chances to win.

campaign was that for all four games, and despite little niggling injuries here and there, the full complement of 26 players was available. That reflected immense credit on the back-room medical and fitness staff, Mr Donald MacLeod, Dr James Robson, Tommy McMullen and David McLean. None of the other countries could make such a claim for a clean bill of health at selection time.

Sadly, the Ivory Coast's final game, in which they lost to Tonga by 29–11, contained that element of tragedy countries who have higher knowledge of fitness and strengthening work and, perhaps, a greater ability to hold on to skill levels under the kind of pressure that modern international rugby imposes. No one can doubt the unfettered joy and satisfaction felt by the entire Ivory Coast squad at having qualified to participate in the World Cup competition proper. That such a thrill should be dampened by a tragedy like this was the great heartbreak of the 1995 World Cup.

MIDLAND

Market Scene, Northern Town, 1939 L. S. Lowry. Courtesy City of Salford Art Gallery.

At work in the community

The communities around our branches are the beneficiaries of substantial funds from our pre-tax profits. There is a strategy to our donations; the majority of them go to projects in the inner cities and to socially-deprived and disabled people. Our staff are also encouraged to raise funds for their own favourite causes and the bank will often help by doubling the proceeds of their efforts. This doesn't just make the community a better place to live. It also makes the bank a better place to work.

The Listening Bank

Member HSBC ⟨X⟩ Group

The Non-qualifiers
Valiant in defeat
Mick Cleary

For most of the countries competing in South Africa there was a predictable end to a journey which had begun almost three years earlier. The likes of the Ivory Coast, Japan, Tonga and, once the draw was made, perhaps even Romania, knew that their World Cup would last no more than ten days. Time enough, though, to pack in a lifetime's experience, to attempt to ward off humiliation and, even in defeat, perhaps to strike out occasionally and irritate the hell out of the big boys.

Of course the name of Max Brito will long hang over the preliminary stage of the World Cup finals. When the Ivory Coast winger was injured in the last pool match against Tonga, the presence of professional paramedics and air transport at pitchside in Rustenburg meant that he had the best possible chance of surviving without disability. Sadly, there was to be no reprieve: his heavy fall resulted in total quadriplegia. Perhaps any future play-offs among the lesser nations in the World Cup might be named in his honour and any monies raised be donated to his trust fund.

As for the team, they acquitted themselves well enough, particularly after the opening 89–0 drubbing by Scotland suggested that they might be on the end of a fearful lashing from the French. While it's true that France came away with a 54–18 victory, the Ivorians at least had the satisfaction of crossing the try-line. In that ill-fated game against Tonga the Ivory Coast put up their best display in losing 29–11. The future for the Africans will be every bit as difficult as the present was here. 'If the International Board don't help the little countries like us, rugby will die,' said their captain, Athanase Dali, during the tournament. 'Only 5,000 people play rugby in the Ivory Coast and the IB must help to bring more people to the game. We cannot play World Cup qualifiers alone. We need experience in the top echelons.' Dali's view was echoed by his coach, Claude Ezoua. 'We need to play to prosper,' said Ezoua. 'Not the likes of England or the Springboks, but the smaller nations, such as Italy and Romania. We proved against France that in Africa beautiful rugby can be produced.' In Pool D Tonga also

The Ivory Coast's Jean Sathicq and captain Athanase Dali pressurise Scotland's Tony Stanger. Flanker Patrice Pere pays close attention. The Ivory Coast played throughout with great credit, but proved that the gap between established and developing rugby-playing nations is as large as ever.

Tonga's Akuila Mafi charges through the Ivory Coast midfield.

achieved the dubious distinction of having the first player to be sent off in the 1995 World Cup when Feleti Mahoni was dismissed and subsequently suspended for six weeks for unlawful use of the boot in the match against France.

If the Ivory Coast think they have problems in finding opposition, then a similar fate may well befall the Japanese after their performances here. Their humiliating 145–17 defeat by New Zealand, and 107 points conceded in all to Wales and Ireland, will make it increasingly difficult for them to persuade any of the leading nations to head their way, even for a warm-up match. This would be a great pity, for even when pinned to the wall in their respective games, the Japanese showed some thrilling glimpses of their handling and running skills when they were able to

Sinali Latu, part of Japan's Tongan trio, in action against Wales. Again, Japan showed that size is everything in modern-day rugby.

Ian Jones outjumps Greg Prosser in the Pool C clash between New Zealand and Wales. For the second tournament in succession Wales failed to get beyond the pool stages of the competition.

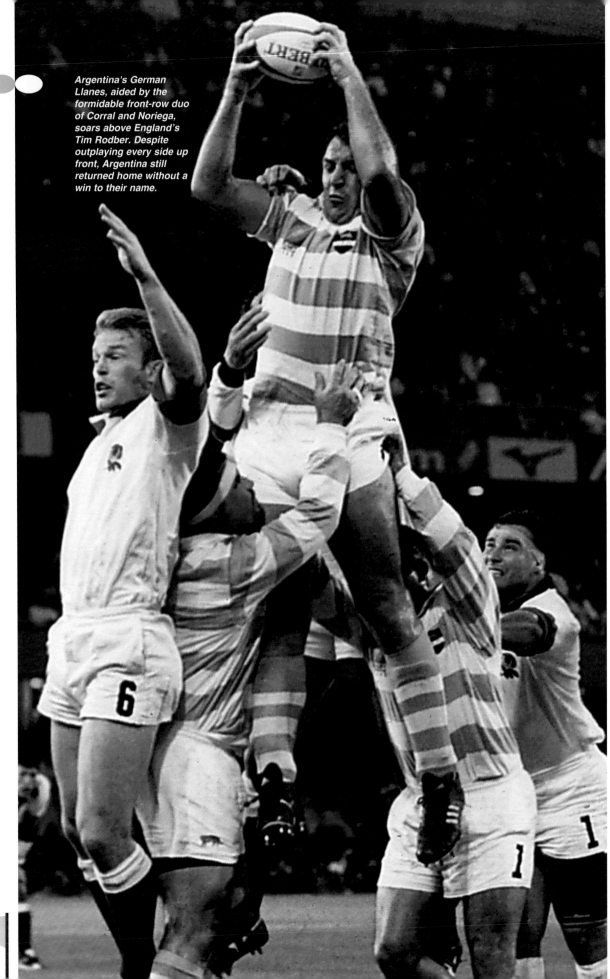

Argentina's German Llanes, aided by the formidable front-row duo of Corral and Noriega, soars above England's Tim Rodber. Despite outplaying every side up front, Argentina still returned home without a win to their name.

Romanian scrum-half Vasile Flutur in action in the Pool A clash with South Africa. The Romanians played with great passion in the so-called 'group of death'.

break out from desperate defence. It's not difficult to see where the difficulty lies. 'Our obvious problems are size and power,' said their manager, Zenzaburo Shirai.

This was the group that was always going to have a decisive last game to determine who went through to the final stages – Wales against Ireland on the last Sunday of the pool round. That there was so much riding on the result was obvious enough: that the two sets of players knew each other so well was also evident. Neither of these factors can explain why the teams produced such a miserably negative match, riddled with errors and serious flaws in attitude. Games should be won by those who dare to reach out, not because one team's nerve is marginally less angst-ridden than the other's. Ireland and Wales staged the worst game of the tournament, Ireland coming through by the narrowest of margins, 24–23, by dint of two early tries from Popplewell and McBride. Wales left it far too late to have a run at Ireland, timidity which might well have cost them victory. 'I just can't understand how our forwards gave away two tries,' said Welsh skipper Mike Hall afterwards. 'It's been a very demanding opening ten days,' was all the Ireland manager, Noel Murphy, would say in mitigation of his side's performance.

The two other pools were both valiantly contested. England's group, which featured Western Samoa, Argentina and Italy, always promised to cause some bruises, if not surprises. As it was England came through, with the bruises, but without ever being allowed to hit any sort of stride. The shock of the group, perhaps, was that Argentina could play in the way they did and still lose all three matches. With Noriega, Mendez, Llanes and Martin to the fore they had the outstanding pack of the

pool, and probably the tournament. Yet for all the promise of the build-up, they just could not finish things off. They must have set a World Cup record for the number of times they dropped the ball with the line at their mercy. They contrived to throw away a 13-point lead in the last 18 minutes against Western Samoa in East London, even failing to win a collapsed scrum award in the very last minute. Against Italy in the final pool match it was the same story: an interception try three minutes from time gave the Italians a 31–25 victory.

The so-called 'group of death' looked as if two of its teams might already be in the mortuary when the competition kicked off. Canada and Romania had both arrived with very threadbare records, and yet, from somewhere, they found the resolve and the method to trouble, in varying degrees, both Australia and South Africa. After the tumult of their opening-day win over Australia, the Springboks were brought rudely back down to earth in their 21–8 victory over Romania. 'We wanted to show everyone the Romanian players were not here as tourists,' said their captain and No. 8, Tiberiu Brinza. 'This common goal was our main motivation and inspiration.'

It was Canada, though, who really set the two qualifiers back on their heels. They let Australia slip away for two early tries but then proceeded to hit them hard for the next 70 minutes, going down eventually by 27–11. It was in Port Elizabeth that the Canadians' natural commitment boiled over, the short-arm punch from behind by Scott Stewart triggering the brawl which saw three players (Gareth Rees and Rod Snow of Canada and James Dalton of South Africa) sent off and two more (Pieter Hendriks and Stewart) later cited. It was a sad way to end their campaign.

Canadian captain Gareth Rees is tackled by Australia's Matt Burke. The World Cup was to end in disgrace for both Rees and the Canadian team.

Ieuan Evans

❛ I honestly thought that we would do quite well in the World Cup. And yet here we are again trying to work out where it all went wrong and where Wales go from here. It's become rather a familiar line of inquiry over the last ten years and I'm not sure we're yet any nearer to finding a lasting solution.

Certainly we need to move the game up to a higher place. We are far too one-dimensional in our attitude, a limitation which cost us dearly against Ireland. New Zealand have shown the way forward with their total, 15-man rugby. They were the best team in the competition, even though South Africa brought some special qualities of their own to the final. The All Blacks had the nerve to go out and play an exciting brand of rugby, not to entertain the crowd but to win matches. They knew that if they could get the ball to their runners, and not just Lomu, they would score tries. They also knew that if they could get the ball out wide they had the man to support and round off the movements in Josh Kronfeld. The openside flanker was my player of the World Cup. He had pace, hands, vision and a sense of opportunism. He was brilliant; he had a quiet game in the final only because his forwards were having problems and he had to wade in and help them out.

New Zealand were fortunate in that they came into the tournament unheralded, and therefore nothing much was expected of them. In contrast, everything was expected of South Africa. If for no other reason, the Springboks deserved their success because they were able to cope with this sort of pressure. If anything I felt that the pressure on myself was off coming into the tournament. There had been a change of coach, which resulted in my losing the captaincy. I had adapted to all this by the time we got to South Africa. The Welsh captaincy had always been an honour to me and never a burden. Even so, it was quite nice in some ways to be just one of the troops again. It meant that you could focus solely on your own game without the distraction of the form of others or dealings with the media.

Training beforehand had been very good, both in Wales and out in Bloemfontein. We quickly got used to altitude, so much so that when we had a live practice session against Orange Free State they were very impressed by our levels of fitness. Things hadn't changed too much under Alex Evans for the simple reason that there is never too much that can be changed. A few faces were different, it's true, but rugby is essentially a simple game. You win the ball first and then you set out to retain it. If you retain it long enough, then you will score. Possession and retention: this is the philosophy of rugby which has been the backbone of the All Blacks for decades. It showed in the way that they played against everyone and in the way Wales played against them.

We gave the ball away and they scored. How simple it all sounds. To make sure it doesn't happen, you have to have the right technical skills as well as the right mental attitude. You also need to be used to playing the game at pace and under pressure. Whatever we may say about our own domestic game, the results prove that we are not playing at a high enough intensity week in, week out. We had a lot of the game against the All Blacks, but in the key areas we were out of it. We let them gallop away to a lead of 20-plus points, which you can't afford to do against any side, let alone the All Blacks. I must say that their rugby in the tournament was a pleasure to watch and you have to feel for them that they did not win. We'd had hopes ourselves of making a mark, particularly after our win over Japan. It was a good opening for us. We very quickly got on top and put a lot of points on the board by half-time but could not completely finish them off. The All Blacks managed it a week later, and perhaps that mental ruthlessness is one of the factors which currently divides us as rugby-playing nations. We simply should have beaten the Japanese, brave as they were in their running and passing, by a far greater margin than we did.

Even so we felt comfortable with ourselves. The camp in Bloemfontein couldn't have been better. We were very well looked after in terms of the facilities made available to us and the warm reception given to us by the locals. Even the All Blacks defeat did not set us back too far. Sure, we ought to have done several things better, but we were in good enough spirits to face Ireland with confidence. But the game itself was pitiful, easily one of the worst matches of the tournament. We had a horrendous start, gifting them two tries in the opening few minutes, and then didn't do enough quickly enough to get back into contention. Against Ireland you have got to dictate the terms and the pace. We did neither. We simply slumped to the floor and only when it was far, far too late did we have the courage to get out there and play some rugby. It was to our discredit that we did not have the nerve to do it sooner. We had over 60 per cent of the game, yet the record books will show that it was Ireland who won and Wales, for the second World Cup in succession, who went home.

We were devastated by the realisation of it all the next morning. Yet again there is much soul-searching, and much mud-slinging, among the Welsh. The game is on the verge of great change with all the money which is flooding into the southern hemisphere. Once again they are setting the pace and we are following behind about five years later. We really have got to sort out exactly what we want to do: compete or just be also-rans. Certainly defeat does not sit comfortably on my shoulders, which is why I shall be carrying on. I would hate to go out on that sort of note. ❯

The expression on Ieuan Evans' face typifies the frustration felt by the vast array of Welsh supporters.

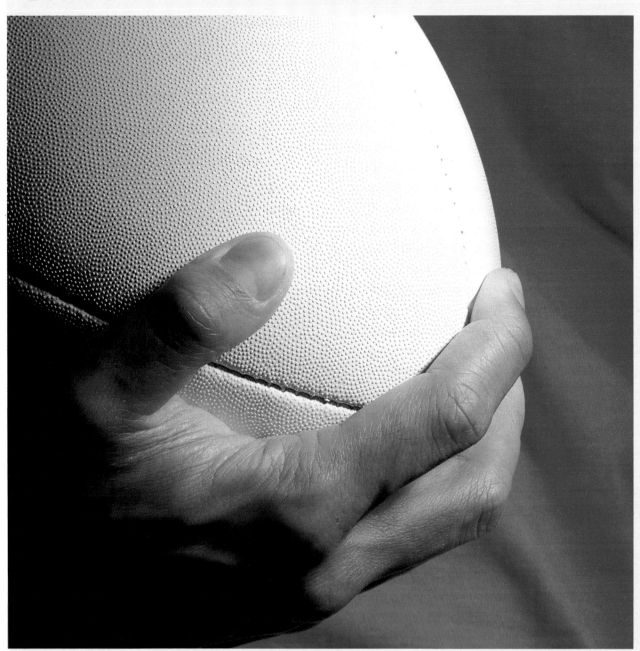

The top players have a number of things in common.

Experience of playing conditions around the world. A capacity to read the game. A sense of teamwork. Strength. Speed. And, above all, the ability to make fast decisions.

HongkongBank

The Hongkong and Shanghai Banking Corporation Limited

Fast decisions. Worldwide.

The Durban Quarter-final
France extinguish legendary Irish fire
Clem Thomas

Many great Irish names had gathered in sub-tropical Durban to see their team attempt to reach the semi-finals of the World Cup for the first time. They included the legendary fly-half Jackie Kyle, who has spent a lifetime as a medical missionary in Zambia, and other worthies of great renown such as Willie John McBride, Sid Millar, Tony O'Reilly, Noel Henderson, Fuzzie Anderson and Tom Kiernan. Even the presence of such august predecessors failed to inspire the Irish, for this turned out to be the poorest of the quarter-finals by some distance, and the worst possible advertisement for the Five Nations Championship.

Because of the cynical nature of the match, it was an indictment of the static European approach to playing rugby. Both teams preferred to concede penalties rather than risk a try being scored. So many players deliberately got offside, thus ruining the flow of the game, that it was surprising the referee, Ed Morrison of England, did not invoke the law concerning persistent infringement. It has to be said that it was the Irish who were the major offenders. Instead of playing their usual sort of 'give it a crack, boys' style of game, they uncharacteristically went into a defensive shell, and, worse still, showed no real ambition to win the World Cup, either by displaying their legendary fire and passion or by any constructive attitude.

Similarly, the French, who, to date, had never looked remotely like posing a realistic challenge to any of the major teams, were curiously subdued and struggled to find any cohesion between their backs and forwards, although their forwards looked miles better than

Eric Elwood, Ireland's fly-half, who kicked all of his side's points in a remarkably subdued performance.

Christophe Deylaud missed two dropped goals for France in the quarter-final clash. In general it was, for him, a disappointing tournament.

previously. That prompted their coach, Pierre Berbizier, to say at the post-match press conference: 'The French team are now close to drinking champagne, but at the moment we are struggling to get the cork out of the bottle.' He went on to comment that the semi-final would not be easy, but that history had proved that France succeed better against southern hemisphere countries, and that the team had improved since the opening game. In comparison the French team manager, Guy Laporte, was less bullish, but he said that although he was much happier with the forwards, there was a lot to be done to improve the link between forwards and backs, because France desired a much more fluent style than they had so far produced. He was, of course, bearing in mind that against neither Scotland nor Ireland had they scored a try until the 79th minute.

Nevertheless, France were through to a semi-final against South Africa while England were to meet New Zealand. It set up the exciting and remarkable possibility of a shift of rugby power from the southern to the northern hemisphere and of an improvement on the European performance in the previous two World Cups, in which only one Five Nations side – France in 1987 and England in 1991 – had reached the final. The prospect was, however, never to be realised: both teams were to bite the dust in the penultimate round – with France having every reason to feel aggrieved – and to meet each other to determine not the championship of the world, but third and fourth places in the rankings.

The final score, 36–12, in the quarter-final (a goal, a try, and eight penalties for France to four penalties by the Irish) was distorted by the fact that the first French try

The omnipresent Abdelatif Benazzi collects the high ball ahead of team-mate Jean-Luc Sadourny and Irish wing Darragh O'Mahony.

The French front row. From left to right: Louis Armary, Jean-Michel Gonzalez and Christian Califano.

A dazed Simon Geoghegan surfaces from a ruck. The Ireland wing, however, showed his class throughout the tournament.

was scored in the 79th minute and the second in the fourth minute of injury time. It was, in truth, an appalling game of rugby in which the cynicism of preventing a try at all costs was reflected in the number of kickable penalties awarded. It allowed Thierry Lacroix to provide a virtuoso display of goal-kicking – eight out of nine penalties – and unceremoniously booted Ireland out of the World Cup, and took the Tricolours a step further towards the final than they had achieved in the last tournament.

The French players had been complaining all week about their the heavy workload in training. Pierre

Berbizier, they said, was the French equivalent of Captain Bligh and worked them too hard. Certainly they looked a jaded side and showed little of their usual elan or attacking flair against what, apart from the mercurial Simon Geoghegan, was a comparatively slow Irish back division. Although the Irish stuck firmly to their usual preoccupation with the garryowen, and provided their early fearsome challenge to those prepared to win a posthumous VC, the French showed great patience and ping-ponged, penalty for penalty, as Eric Elwood and Lacroix kicked four each before half-time.

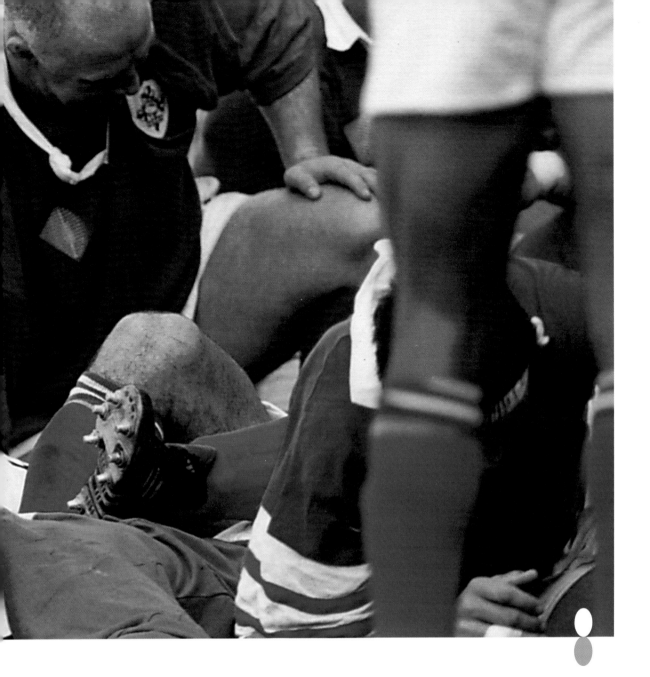

The first half qualified as perhaps the most boring of the tournament so far as France, poorly served at half-back, looked tired and allowed the Irish to drag them down to their own level of mediocrity in attack. There was scarcely a flash of running rugby and, apart from the penalties, there was hardly an incident worth recording. It was ironic that the only decent run by the French in that first half came from the monstrous Olivier Merle, who made a remarkable side-stepping run to set up the last French score before the interval. Christophe Deylaud missed a simple dropped goal, but, surprise,

surprise, Ireland were offside and Lacroix kicked the sitter.

Meanwhile, the French continued to win overwhelming possession in the line-outs and the loose play, but got nowhere against the relentless spoiling of the Irish defence. It is a tragedy when a great game like rugby football is diminished by the attitudes of the players, particularly when they are being observed by such a massive worldwide audience. To allow players of the quality of Simon Geoghegan and Emile Ntamack to languish with barely a pass in the whole game was criminal

Darragh O'Mahony, the Ireland wing, tries to shrug off the challenge of Abdelatif Benazzi and Christophe Deylaud during one of the livelier moments of the match for Ireland.

folly and a denial of the spirit of the game. It was difficult to understand why both teams had, apparently, developed a philosophy of not wanting to lose at any price.

One expected more of France, of all people, for no country performs greater deeds of derring-do or shows more running flair than they. Their strange reluctance to run the ball at the Irish was a mystery. However, in the second half, it was the French forwards who finally took control of the game. They stepped up the pace and the possession and again it was a thrust by Merle which finally saw France take the lead, for the first time, some seven minutes after the interval. Once again, the first concerted attack of the game was cynically stifled by the concession of a penalty for offside and Lacroix made no mistake with the kick. A couple of minutes later, he kicked another and the French began to breathe a little easier.

From hereon there was no doubt as to who were the masters. France won the ball at will and the Irish defence slowly began to crumble. Ireland then lost Gabriel Fulcher, who was replaced by Eddie Halvey, but the increasing pressure saw them concede still more penalties. Lacroix continued to punish them by succeeding with two more. Ireland were undone by 24–12 as the game went into the 80th minute. The try famine ended when Olivier Roumat made a charge into the Irish 22 and Deylaud made his only contribution to the game by popping up the ball for Saint-André to score near the posts. Lacroix converted for a personal tally of 26 points in the match. Finally, in the fourth minute of injury time, the French hammered home their undoubted supremacy when their flying wing Emile Ntamack intercepted a pass by Brendan Mullin near his own try-line and raced some 95 yards to score.

What they said . . .

Philippe Saint-André: 'I am satisfied with my side's performance. We wanted to make sure we got through to the semis; we must kick better if we want to win the tournament. We played well in the second half, but did not score enough tries. I think we have a good chance to get through to the finals.'

Terry Kingston: 'We played well in the first half; the French got too much ball in the second. We could not plug all the gaps. We defended well in the first half, but we did not use all our opportunities. The French got too much ball in the line-outs. We did not have an answer to that. It was very hot – but for both teams. We were glad to be in the quarter-finals. We should have liked to have got further, but the French were too strong.'

Pierre Berbizier: 'We were there [in the final] in 1987 and we want to go that one step further. We will definitely work on the mistakes we made today, for instance our handling of the ball, but that is not serious.'

Philippe Saint-André, the French captain, celebrates his quarter-final try along with Emile Ntamack and Thierry Lacroix.

Simon Geoghegan

❛ We'd had a poor Five Nations and lost to Italy in a warm-up match, yet we arrived at the World Cup in decent spirits. Such is the optimism of the Irish. Unfortunately, it may not sustain us for much longer. We can always point to the unexpected performances, such as the one against Australia in the quarter-final of the 1991 World Cup, to support the view that we are capable of beating anyone on our day. Prior to that tournament, too, we had had a rotten Five Nations and even lost to Gloucester in a warm-up match, which is why we weren't too despondent this time round. But after this World Cup I believe that unless we completely reorganise our set-up, and significantly change our attitude in Ireland, then we will never be able to compete with the big boys. If we were to play South Africa, Australia and New Zealand ten times then we would lose every time.

Our club rugby is just nowhere near the right sort of standard to be considered adequate preparation for the

Battered and bloodied, Simon Geoghegan assesses the damage during Ireland's Pool C decider against Wales.

international game. We are simply not on a level playing field with the others. All-Ireland League rugby is, at best, roughly equivalent to Division 2 of the Courage Leagues in England. Several of the teams in the the English Leagues are hanging on by their fingernails too, in my opinion.

None of this is meant to be whingeing: it is an objective appraisal of what we need to do. The game has moved on enormously since the last World Cup. Ireland, and Wales for that matter, have genuinely to decide whether they want to move with it or just make up the numbers at the next World Cup. As it stands, the clubs are far too powerful in determining the structure of the game in Ireland, and what style of rugby should be played. The days of stodgy old set-piece play, with the hope of getting a few penalty opportunities, are over. If Ireland is to step up to the necessary level they have to play more dynamic rugby.

Maybe they need to look outside the country for a coaching panel. All the coaches in the AIL are fairly well set on playing a ten-man game. It would be ludicrous to expect them, or the players, to suddenly switch to a totally different and alien style when they pull on an Ireland shirt. Whether we like it or not, there is a distinct difference between run-of-the-mill first-class rugby and international rugby. You have to consider the elite game as a separate entity. It may be that people will decide that the change is not worth it, but whatever the feeling, they must address the issue and all its implications. It would certainly make rugby even more of a full-time pursuit than it is already. Again, there are no easy solutions here, but at least let's get a serious debate going. We owe it to the young players coming through at the moment – we have got to start giving them some hope.

Some people might think we had a reasonable World Cup in that we gave the All Blacks a match, defeated Wales and so finished as one of the top eight nations. The way I see it, we beat only two countries – Wales and Japan – and were seen off for the umpteenth time by the French. If we'd been in England's group, alongside Western Samoa, Italy and Argentina, I don't think we would have qualified. Our best effort was in the first match against New Zealand. We were competitive and in contention and would have remained so right through to the final whistle if we hadn't given away two soft tries at the end of the first half. This match was always going to be our best chance to make our mark. They were coming at it new and untested, whereas we had had our season plus a fortnight together. That preparation time makes all

the difference to an Irish team. It's so hard to get together during the Championship. For those of us living in England, by the time we fly over to Dublin and find our feet the match is upon us. Here we had a chance to get physically fit and mentally focused, and I think the benefits showed. We had a great opening 20 minutes, which set the All blacks back on their heels. If it hadn't been for Lomu and our mistakes, we would have been right in there with a shout.

We did make mistakes, though, and they did have Lomu. He is some freak. The South Africans handled him well, but generally, no matter what you do to close him down, he still manages to at least half break the first tackle. You have to be spot-on mentally and technically if you are going to bring him down. James Small was obviously in the right frame of mind, for he dealt with him well. Lomu was without a doubt the player of the tournament. He looked as if he might be caught out completely on his defence, but he learned quickly, and by the time he came face to face with Tony Underwood he knew what to do. Both Ireland's Richard Wallace and Scotland's Craig Joiner were able to leave him for dead on a couple of occasions in their matches. By the England game, though, Lomu had learned to position himself between the outside centre and winger, rather than head-on, so that he did not have to turn and chase for the tackle from a flat-footed position. He is fast, strong and has a hell of a hand-off. Like Va'aiga Tuigamala, he carries his hands very low when he runs so you get the full force if you try to tackle him round the waist. You've either got to swamp him, as South Africa did, or take him very low indeed.

The Japan game was always going to be difficult for us. We almost inevitably switched off after the New Zealand match. Still, we got through with no injuries, which was the important thing. The Japanese, even though they were badly beaten by the Blacks, showed the world a thing or two about handling and running. The Wales game was a very tense affair. I was sure we'd win, but nonetheless it ended up a bit of a struggle. It highlighted the difficulties both countries face.

The quarter-final against France was a disappointment for me personally in that I woke up on Friday with a virus. Denis McBride also had problems, as did one or two others. We didn't play the right game against the French, either. We should have done more than just take them on up front and hope to kick a few goals. In short, that must be the lesson we take away from this tournament. Ireland must adapt, or we will continue to be up against it. **"**

Instant reaction

NEXT

NEXT SHOPPING AVAILABLE IN STORE OR THROUGH THE NEXT DIRECTORY.
PHONE 0345 100 500, 8AM-11PM LOCAL RATE, TO APPLY FOR YOUR COPY.

0345 100 500

The Johannesburg Quarter-final
Chester's triumphant return
Bill McLaren

The quarter-final at Ellis Park, Johannesburg between South Africa and Western Samoa was an intriguing prospect which brought from the South African camp concern about the intimidating tackling of the Pacific Islanders and their capacity for striking unexpectedly out of defence in a manner reminiscent of the French and the Fijians.

Apart from their heartening defeat (27–18) of the reigning world champions, Australia, in the opening match of the tournament, the South Africans had found it hard to achieve any consistent rhythm, and apart from the strength and pace of Joost van der Westhuizen, they lacked incision, a fact borne out by their disappointing haul of only six tries to three conceded. Of course, their second game against Romania was always likely to be hard going, for the Romanians are past masters at stopping their opponents from playing and, as it turned out, they played out of their skins against the host country. Nor were Canada an easy ride, and it took massive forward power, resulting in two tries by Adriaan Richter, converted by Joel Stransky, and two penalty goals from Stransky to give South Africa a 20–0 win in a contest marked in particular by one unholy punch-up that ended up with three players being dismissed.

Western Samoa had seen off the Italians 48–18, squeezed through by 32–26 over the Argentinians, who had a good Cup run, then lost 44–22 to England, for whom Jonathan Callard scored 21 points with five penalty goals and three conversions. The Samoans were desperately keen to go one better than in 1991, when they lost in the quarter-final to Scotland, and they once again had respected back-up in manager Bryan Williams, the former New Zealand wing, and coach Peter Schuster.

As it turned out, South Africa won with a bit to spare. Indeed, they led by 35–0 after 46 minutes and only when they eased off did the Samoans make a match of it. Perhaps the biggest concern after the game, which South Africa eventually won by 42–14, was the catalogue of injuries suffered by the home players. The most serious was the broken hand bone sustained by that gifted full-back André Joubert, who was replaced by Brendan

Venter with Gavin Johnson moving back as last line. Ruben Kruger, Mark Andrews and Kobus Wiese all departed the scene and there was the unusual sight of a hooker replacing a lock forward when Naka Drotské (who had been introduced to the South African squad following James Dalton's ban after the match against Canada) came on for Wiese.

One of the tackles by the Samoan full-back Mike Umaga, who played a season in Scotland with Glasgow High/Kelvinside, raised much controversy. It laid out Van der Westhuizen with a face injury. That was not the only

Down and out. Joost van der Westhuizen lies motionless after being flattened by a Michael Umaga tackle. The ferocious nature of the Western Samoan tackling caused great controversy.

high big hit in the game: Andrews suffered rib damage when he was shoulder-charged by Lio Falaniko, who drove up the side of the maul in an offside position with Andrews defenceless. It is high time that the International Board stipulated what constitutes a dangerous tackle. Of course, referees are empowered to make such judgements, but they need some guidance in black and white so that there can be no doubt about what is permissible and what is not. The Pacific Islands in particular relish the physical aspect of tackling, and one of the aims in going high is to dislodge the ball with a view to spawning a counter-attack. But clearly there are occasions when the tackle is meant to hurt or injure, as in the case of Van der Westhuizen, who prodded the ball through with deft footwork and then was hit high and late. The law states that anything above shoulder height constitutes

François Pienaar, the influential South African captain, leads his team's charge against Fata Sini, the Samoan fly-half.

a high tackle, but some tackles below that can be seriously damaging. To the credit of the World Cup committee, Umaga was cited for dangerous tackling and banned for 90 days, subsequently reduced to 60 days. It is also disappointing that referees take no action against players who grab an opponent by the legs, lift him upwards off the ground and then turn him before dumping him on the ground like a sack of potatoes. If this is not dangerous tackling I don't know what is, and the practice should be outlawed before someone is very badly injured or even worse.

The Western Samoans certainly gained no friends with their cynical adherence to the occasional dangerous tackle, and that is a pity, because there is no doubt that they are among the most attractive counter-attackers in the game. That was one aspect of their play that concerned the South Africans, because when bulky, determined Pacific Islanders decide to run from deep, they can be very hard to put on the floor. They had players of great stature. Brian Lima is a hefty wing with try-scoring potential, as all those who have seen him captivate the Hong Kong Sevens audience will know. To'o

Vaega is a nippy, creative midfield player and George Harder was another wing in the Lima mould. Fata Sini at fly-half has the build of a prop. He had shattered England with two cracking late tries, one the result of a power-packed thrust through some four English tackles – and he only got into the game at all as an injury replacement. Such was the strength of Western Samoa's tight five forwards that the exalted giant Peter Fatialofa was consigned to the bench. They appreciated the need to have a well-balanced cover forward, too. In Shem Tatupu, Pat Lam and Peter Junior Paramore they had just that. Lam took over as captain and Tatupu proved to be a highly productive forager and finisher.

The Samoans did very well at the set positions, taking one ball against the scrummage put-in and sharing the line-outs with the distinguished trio of Wiese, Andrews and Rudolf Straeuli. But in the concession of penalties, South Africa proved far more aware and disciplined. They received 18 offence kicks to only eight by the Samoans, and this contributed to a handsome territorial advantage to the host country. Although he was injured on more than one occasion, Van der Westhuizen provided more evidence of why South Africans rate him as the best scrum-half in the world. That perhaps pitches it a bit too high, but he is certainly a wonderfully exciting player with the static strength to stay on his feet in the tackles, a strong body which is hard to arrest and an edge of pace which can catch opposing defenders by surprise. He also is capable of running with a low carriage rather in the manner that has made Scotland's Gary Armstrong such a difficult little man to catch. Van der Westhuizen frequently ducked under tackles, and although he never looked like aspiring to the 11 tries he scored on the tour of Australia in 1993, he was the spark plug to many of the South African attack plays and also asked questions himself of

another during the Springboks' tour of the United Kingdom in 1994, he suffered hamstring damage which precluded him from the World Cup squad. In fact Williams himself made the decision to pull out, a brave act, because he did not want to let down his colleagues by risking breakdown. His standing in South African sporting circles was never more startlingly illustrated than at the opening game between South Africa and Australia at Newlands in Cape Town. Williams, one of the Western Province organising committee, climbed the stairs to the media area to ensure that all was well. No sooner had he been recognised than the entire population of the enclosure at the front of the main West Stand, almost all

The jet-propelled Kobus Wiese clears the melee to win a line-out for South Africa.

opposing fringe defenders.

The match was a personal triumph for the black wing Chester Williams. He had become something of a folk hero in South Africa's new atmosphere of a united people and one nation. Having played 11 internationals in a row since his first cap against Argentina in 1993, when he scored a try, and having charmed one audience after

of them whites, stood, turned and looked upwards to where he was. They clapped and clapped for what seemed an age. It was a touching tribute to a gifted black player. Of course, Williams was desperately keen to get back into action, but his place had gone to Pieter Hendriks, who had scored an important try against Australia. When I asked Williams if he was fit again and he

The South African fans celebrate the return of Chester Williams.

Chester Williams dives over the Samoan line to score his fourth try of the match.

assured me that he was, I jokingly suggested that I might kick either James Small or Hendriks in the ankle to allow him to join the squad. His eyes twinkled at the prospect. As things turned out, of course, the ban on Hendriks after the brawl against Canada opened the door for Williams for the quarter-final.

Against Western Samoa, Williams roared in for four

Chester Williams sprints beyond the reach of Western Samoan flanker Shem Tatupu.

tries, two of which admittedly were somewhat doubtful, but all of which gave immense pleasure to South African rugby folk, who acknowledge him, black and white alike, as one of their own and of whom they are very proud. Williams in full flight is a joy to behold. He is quick but elegant with it, a silken runner who always seems to have a little left in the tank; his skill levels are high and he is sound in defence as well.

South Africa's other tries were scored by Mark Andrews and Chris Rossouw, who was making quite an impact as successor to the inimitable Uli Schmidt. Gavin Johnson weighed in with two penalty goals and three conversions. The Western Samoan tries were by Tu'etu Nu'uali'itia and Tatupu, each converted by Topo Fa'amasino.

So Western Samoa departed the scene, having reached a place in the quarter-finals but having also alerted the game's legislators to the growing tendency to indulge in dangerous tackling. Another passing thought was what course of action would have been open to the South Africans if a fifth player had left the field injured. The law states that only four may be replaced. One wonders why, unless the aim is to discourage the sharp practice of using replacements for tactical reasons rather than because of injury.

Although South Africa's comprehensive victory was achieved at a cost, all four of the injured players were available for the semi-final game against France.

What they said . . .

Brian Williams: 'We had high hopes and aspirations to go far. We made the last eight in 1991 but we hoped to go one further this time. It does prove that 1991 was not a fluke and we shall move on to bigger and better things.'

François Pienaar: 'I'm delighted to say we peaked for the second time in the tournament to score a good win against very difficult opponents. We played well against Australia in the opening match, but then we were not really at our best in beating Romania and Canada. I felt we were in control against Western Samoa from the start. Our line-out was much better and our discipline was excellent – we hardly conceded any penalties in the whole match. It was good to score six tries because they are tremendous tacklers. They are a very physical side, and I just hope Joost van der Westhuizen and André Joubert are fit for the semi-finals. They both took crunching tackles. We have a week to recover before we play France, and we are just one win away from the World Cup final.'

Western Samoa's captain, Pat Lam, leads by example. The victim of the fierce tackle on this occasion is South Africa's Japie Mulder.

England's Brian Moore contemplates the task confronting England in their quarter-final clash against Australia.

The Cape Town Quarter-final
Rob's boot puts out the holders
Stephen Jones

Jeremy Guscott can justly claim to have played a part in two of the great drop-kicking moments the game has seen – as a first-on-the-scene spectator. It was Guscott who was the first to congratulate Stuart Barnes, his colleague at Bath, when Barnes drilled over the fantastic kick which won England's Pilkington Cup in 1992 in the last seconds of the second period of extra time. Guscott is not known for demonstrative behaviour on the field, but on this occasion he could hardly contain himself, almost leaping on to Barnes' back as the kick was signalled good. And at Newlands, on a day of massive confrontation and unbearable tension in the quarter-final, there he was again. Rob Andrew had launched a massive drop at goal in the dying seconds of the match, with the score at 22–22 and extra time inexorably creeping up on two exhausted, battered and desperate teams. Andrew watched the ball keenly, as some golfers watch every yard of a drive they are anxious about, while others hit the ball, pick up their tees and walk on, secure in the knowledge that the shot

is good. Guscott had no doubts. He was already jumping on Andrew as the large English contingent in the Newlands stands prepared to go barmy.

Records are meant to be broken, and legends are meant to be superseded. Andrew's kick lasted less than two weeks as the world's most famous dropped goal, because no doubt Joel Stransky's extra-time effort in the final now takes pride of place. But for a heady afternoon and evening – an evening in which every England follower in Cape Town celebrated long and hard – Andrew and England held the crown.

It was an extraordinary match. It had loomed as one of the occasions of the whole tournament ever since we examined the draw and found, months before the event began, that but for a real shock result, either Australia or South Africa would play England in the quarter-final, impossibly early for teams of such high aspirations and such an overwhelmingly tough period of preparation. After South Africa beat Australia in the opening match, it

Dewi Morris terrorises his opposite number, George Gregan. Defensively, the England scrum-half was superb throughout the game.

Will Carling on a familiar midfield charge. The England captain confirmed his return to form during the course of the competition.

'You cannot be serious!' Dewi Morris pleads with referee David Bishop – to no avail as the Australians take a 19-16 lead with only a few minutes remaining.

was Australia who arrived in Cape Town for the quarter-final showdown.

If you can learn anything from body language, then you learned that England were more wound up (as it turned out, in a constructive sort of way) than at any time in the history of this current team. Dewi Morris, who quite rightly had wrested the position at scrum-half from Kyran Bracken, gesticulated to the gatherings of England supporters to try to get them to turn up the volume. The initial momentum was partly dissipated by an early injury to Dean Richards. As the England replacements sat halfway back in the stands, and as there was also some bureaucratic interference, it took ages to get Steve Ojomoh, the temporary replacement, on to the field.

But if the match never exploded into pyrotechnics, then it was still a fantastically compelling affair. There was a tremendous line-out battle between Martin Bayfield and Martin Johnson of England, plus their chief seconds, and Rod McCall and John Eales of Australia and supporting cast. For so long it was effectively leap for leap, both teams sewing up their own ball. Only in one short period of Australian supremacy did the England line-out appear to falter, losing three or four balls on their own throw-in in relatively quick succession. Only days later did a rather rueful Bayfield reveal the secret of the England lapse. The Australians had somehow cottoned on to the English line-out signals, and until England changed the codes, the Australians knew precisely where the ball was to be thrown, a priceless advantage and one from which the estimable Bayfield did extremely well to recover. He was to have his time in the last few seconds.

Michael Lynagh, the Australian captain, opened the scoring after a barge in the line-out from the repaired Richards. However, by the ninth minute Andrew had put over two penalties to take England to 6–3. There also came an instructive moment after 16 minutes, when England put together a series of concerted plays and two or three separate loose balls – disappointingly, Andrew meekly dropped for goal. It was to be a feature of the match that England failed to strike out even when their own good initial play had opened up spaces. It was not a feature which was to cost them the game, but it was a harbinger of some extremely poor responses when they tried to find the accelerator in the semi-final. Later in the match, after the England move of the match had taken the ball through four or five phases, Will Carling lamely kicked the ball and, as he was honest enough to admit later, it was the wrong option both tactically and psychologically.

Yet England received a massive boost after 21 minutes. The Australians tried an inventive back move in the England third of the field and it broke down around Lynagh. England seized the loose ball, Jeremy Guscott sent Tony Underwood sprinting away and Underwood, carving his way down the right wing, outflanked the defence and worked his way half round to the posts. Andrew kicked the goal and it was 13–3. Andrew did miss a penalty after 26 minutes, but it was a sticky period for Australia and Lynagh steadied them only on the stroke of half-time with a penalty. So the score was 13–6 at half-time, a handy lead, but there was no one in Newlands who felt that the game was over.

It was Australia's third quarter, by far. They scored the try essential to their mental wellbeing right at the start of the second half. Lynagh put up a tremendous kick which began its descent between Tony Underwood and Mike Catt, the England full-back. There was some confusion as Underwood appeared to be going for the ball, then apparently stood aside for Catt. Damian Smith made them pay for their hesitation. He leaped, took the kick brilliantly on the full and forced his way over the line. Lynagh kicked a superb goal and the betting at that stage was that the holders would survive. England did regain the lead after 45 minutes, when their forwards hammered towards the Australian line in a rolling maul, which Australia gratefully pulled down. Andrew's three points were useful enough, even if there was something of the professional foul about the way Australia had stopped the drive.

Yet as the match entered the final quarter Australia were leading by 19–16 with two more penalties by Lynagh. The second of these was awarded against Dewi Morris for offside around a scrum. Morris had done a superb job in defence all afternoon, notably in twice pulling down the dangerous Willie Ofahengaue from behind to stop the Australian flanker from crossing the advantage line. This time, he was just too quick to be true.

Again, an Andrew penalty goal brought England level when Australia obstructed at the England kick-off after Lynagh's penalty. Again, as the tension increased, Lynagh kicked Australia ahead. With six minutes remaining, and with Mike Catt having missed badly with what he had hoped would be the saving drop-kick. Andrew brought England level again with his sixth successful kick of the match. It was only from shortish range, but at that stage of the match and the competition, there were no easy kicks and his steely nerves held up brilliantly.

Extra time loomed ever larger. Then England were given a penalty in their own half and a touch-finder set them up with a line-out on the left-hand side of the field, near the Australian 10-metre line. It had to be the perfect throw from Brian Moore. It was. Bayfield took it near the top of his jump. Victor Ubogu drove in and the rest of the forwards set up a driving maul. It was to have the same effect as American footballers trying to get within field-goal range. The maul rumbled onwards, and as Bayfield himself reported afterwards, the Australians were desperately trying to bring it all crashing to earth. There were a few more touches on the tiller, then the ball was sent back from Morris to Andrew and the kick of Andrew's life put England back into the lead.

There was still some desperate English defending in the few remaining seconds as the Australians tried to run the ball from deep positions, only to find the England defence superbly well organised. There was one last relieving chip over the top from Morris and the final whistle went. It was revenge for England for their defeat in the 1991 final. We did not know then, as the players celebrated, that this would be the high point of England's tournament; that they were never to be half so effective again.

But they did prove their courage and ability in a one-off game, their steady nerves under pressure. And they proved that, even if a dropped goal is sometimes deemed to be overvalued at three points, some dropped goals do deserve to win a match.

England flanker Ben Clarke pressurises the Australian defence. Meanwhile, Australia's Matt Burke prepares himself for the crunch.

The kick that put England through to the semi-finals. Little did they know that this was to be the high point of their tournament.

'Have you heard?' Will Carling spreads the good news.

We did it! England's try-scorer Tony Underwood celebrates with team-mate Jeremy Guscott after the game.

What they said . . .

Rob Andrew: 'I gave it everything, but needed to watch the ball all the way because it was drifting right. Mind you, the equalising penalty was more nerve-racking. This England squad have had some great games together and this was another for the list.'

Will Carling: 'That was the greatest game I have played in and I have never seen anything like Rob's kick. After the match he touched Dewi's bruised leg and cured it and later in the evening we found him having a walk in Cape Town Harbour.'

Jack Rowell: 'I had to challenge myself to stay in my seat and not go for a walk behind the stand, as I used to when I was Bath coach. I asked the players to be up for the event, so I could hardly quit the scene of amazing action when it mattered. It must be an extra-special result when the president of the Rugby Union kisses the England captain. I have the video.'

Bob Dwyer: 'When teams play England they often end up wondering "How did they beat us?" Well, in our case it was the combination of the rolling maul and Andrew's kicking. It's up to each nation to play the way they want, but I don't like England's style and I don't find it exciting.

Mind you, they have changed. They kick the ball up the middle rather than to the corners. On balance I think their 1991 side were superior.'

Australian coach Bob Dwyer, deep in thought. His side could not match their heroic feats of 1991.

England coach Jack Rowell passing the time with the press corps.

Coopers & Lybrand

...another great conversion

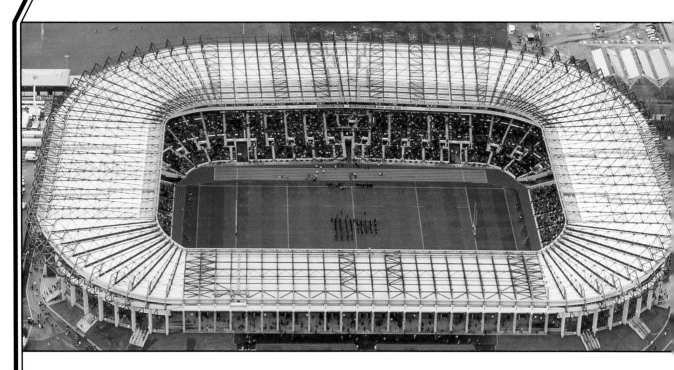

Coopers & Lybrand is delighted to have assisted the Scottish Rugby Union with their successful £36.75 million issue of debentures and the conversion of Murrayfield into a world class rugby stadium.

**Solutions
for Business**

The Pretoria Quarter-final
Scotland battle bravely against the odds
Bill McLaren

The Scots were in no doubt about the size of the task they faced against an All Black side which seemed to the jaundiced eye to act and react just a split-second faster than their rivals and who seemed to have unearthed two new Grant Foxes in Andrew Mehrtens and Simon Culhane. Not only that, but Glen Osborne, the nephew of the great Bill Osborne, midfield All Black of the 1976–82 era from Wanganui, had already shown signs that he was another John Gallagher in the making at full-back. In place of the legendary Michael Jones, New Zealand also placed

before an admiring public a flanker called Josh Kronfeld, a buzz-bomb of a player who covered the paddock like an avenging demon. Of course, there were the old warhorses – Olo Brown, Sean Fitzpatrick, who would be playing in his 66th international, Ian Jones and the inimitable Zinzan Brooke, in my view the most skilful and tactically alert forward I have ever seen – not to mention those North Harbour midfield colleagues Frank Bunce and Walter Little, who had 55 caps between them.

One chink of light for the Scots was that, in the

Jeff Wilson, the young New Zealand wing, had an uncertain afternoon deputising at full-back. Here he fails to hold on to yet another aerial 'bomb'.

Andrew Mehrtens, the New Zealand fly-
kicks for position. The 22-year-old had a
exceptional tournament, leading the exper
believe that, at last, the All Blacks had fou
replacement for Grant

Gavin Hastings slots a penalty to keep the Scots in touch.

Josh Kronfeld was one of the forwards of the tournament. Wherever the ball was, the New Zealand flanker was close by.

absence of Osborne through ankle damage, Jeff Wilson – who had won all six of his caps as a right wing – was shifted to full-back and the top try-scorer in the World Cup, Marc Ellis (with seven), was drafted into the right wing berth. The Scots hoped to unsettle the 21-year-old Wilson with some high-altitude bombing from Chalmers, but New Zealand coach Laurie Mains had no fears for the youngster. Wilson had played much of his provincial rugby as a full-back; he had come to the World Cup as New Zealand's second choice in that position and the lad himself preferred it. In the event Wilson had a dodgy day with his hands, but his mistakes were not fatal ones.

Conscious of the fact that they had never beaten the All Blacks in 17 starts – draws in 1964 (0–0) and 1983 (25–25) were all they had to show – the Scots picked Shiel and Scott Hastings at centre, even though Shiel had damaged his nose cartilage in the French match. It said much for the young Melrose centre's courage that, although the nose was tender to the touch, he never once held back and confirmed his good form of the Cup. Scotland also took a gamble on Damian Cronin. The big fellow wasn't at a peak of fitness because of injury but his experience was so valuable that he was paired with

*An all-too-familiar sight during the course of the World
Cup. Jonah Lomu demolishes the Scottish defence as
he thunders towards the line.*

Doddie Weir for the eighth time. As it turned out, Cronin had to be replaced during the game by Stewart Campbell, who thus gained his eighth cap.

There were those who felt that, as well as searching out Wilson's high-ball capability, Scotland also could get at young Mehrtens, but that theory took little account of either that young fellow's skill and artistry or the manner in which two more experienced colleagues protected him from all ills. Mehrtens operated at the end of the fastest service in the World Cup, Graeme Bachop having such quick hands that the ball was just a blur in its passage. There was in prospect a right royal confrontation between two particularly well-equipped breakaway units – Wainwright, Peters and Morrison against Jamie Joseph, Brooke and Kronfeld. On the day before the game Laurie Mains told me that New Zealand's backs were at the peak of their powers and were just straining at the leash to get into action. They would not hug the touchline, nor would they play aerial ping-pong if there were opportunities for spinning the ball. He was as good as his word: the All Blacks played some gorgeous handling rugby and five of their six tries were scored by their backs. The one that brought home to the Scots that this was not to be their day was Little's second, just after half-time. New Zealand led by only 17–9 at the break but within a minute of the restart Mehrtens hoisted a huge up-and-under, Gavin Hastings had the ball dislodged from his grasp and Little scuttled in off a friendly bounce with not a hand laid on him. The conversion by Mehrtens made it 24–9 and virtually all Scottish hope evaporated. It was then that the 22-year-old fly-half demonstrated another weapon in his armoury: scalding pace. He shot up the right touchline like a super-charged sprinter for a spectacular try which he even had the audacity to convert from the touchline.

The three first-half penalty goals by Gavin Hastings had kept the Scots in contention for long enough and it

*Doddie Weir out-jumps Ian Jones.
It was a good day for the Scot as
he went on to score two tries during
Scotland's final rally.*

*Jonah Lomu pushes his way past Scott
Hastings to score yet another try.*

was to their eternal credit that they staged a mighty rally for the first of Doddie Weir's two tries, converted by his captain. But no sooner had Scottish hopes been revived than the sheer power and pace of the All Blacks killed them again. Little scored his second try, Bunce had already registered his 14th in a New Zealand cap international and captain Sean Fitzpatrick rang down the curtain on New Zealand try-scoring by patiently waiting out on the left touchline while his mates swung the ball to the right, then back to the left again, for him to score. Yet the Scots came again with a drive-over try from Weir, his

*Gavin Hastings contemplates the end of his
ten-year career in international rugby.*

second of the afternoon, and one by Scott Hastings, whose brother finished the game with three penalty goals and three conversions – 104 points in four games. Mehrtens contributed 23 points to New Zealand's 48–30 win.

Of course, the player to make the heaviest impact was Jonah Lomu. The first time he received the ball, the 20-year-old 19st giant took off past Craig Joiner, Scott Hastings and Gavin Hastings with some power and pace. He had yet to be tested in defence, but with ball in hand he was formidable and only the most determined and copybook tackling would torpedo him.

Despite their defeat, the Scots enhanced their reputation as a side with organisation and fighting spirit. They took their defeat in good heart. They had gone down to the stronger side while battling bravely against the odds, and in the process they had registered three tries against the All Blacks and had equalled Australia's record, set in Auckland in 1978, for points scored against New Zealand.

There was sadness, too, in that Scotland's exit from the 1995 World Cup marked the end of the international careers of Gavin Hastings, Ken Milne and Iain Morrison, as well as that of Scotland's team manager, Duncan Paterson, and coach Douglas Morgan. All of them have given massive service to Rugby Union in Scotland and elsewhere. They will not be easily replaced.

What they said . . .

Sean Fitzpatrick: 'Gavin Hastings is the best full-back in the world. He has made a tremendous contribution to rugby, not only in Scotland but to rugby as a whole.'

Andy Irvine: 'With only four sides left in the World Cup now, I have to say that the All Blacks have looked the best team in the tournament so far and must be favourites at this stage to win the Cup… The All Blacks played some brilliant rugby in the first hour to build up a big lead and they looked unstoppable. It was wonderful 15-man rugby – almost seven-a-side rugby at times – which was a tremendous example to the millions of schoolkids watching on TV. They have shown how rugby can and should be played.'

Gavin Hastings: 'Games against New Zealand don't get any easier and we made it hard for ourselves by giving away a couple of soft tries… It's incredible to think we've scored 30 points against New Zealand, including three tries, and yet we've still failed to become the first Scottish side in history to beat them. I had desperately wanted to win this game but at least we can take some consolation from our fightback in the second half. I was very proud of the team. But that's it for me. I have just played my last game of international rugby and I know the time is right to retire. I can honestly say I have enjoyed every minute of my ten years with Scotland, but it's time to move on.'

Sean Fitzpatrick scores New Zealand's final try against the Scots in their quarter-final clash.

Gavin Hastings

❛ I never had any doubts that I would be fit and in the right sort of form to lead Scotland into the World Cup. Likewise, I never had any doubts that we would acquit ourselves well once we were actually there. This may all have seemed unduly optimistic way back last November, just after we had been badly beaten by South Africa at Murrayfield in a game in which I myself played poorly, but I knew the truth of the matter. Scotland is a small rugby-playing country and needs everything to be going in its favour if it is to compete at the highest level. When the Springboks came to us we had barely played any rugby of note in the season. Club rugby in Scotland is no preparation for the international game. So it was no great surprise that we were not able to hold the 'Boks. But with the changes in selection and the long, very structured, preparation time, we were in great shape when the time came to leave for South Africa and the World Cup.

I think that showed in our performances. We played some fine rugby, showing plenty of spirit in the close quarters as well as mobility round the field. In the end we were done in the very last minute by France in our pool game. We then made too many basic mistakes against New Zealand in the quarter-final to have a chance of holding what was an excellent side. So we were beaten, but we bowed out with pride, crossing the All Black line for three tries.

So how did this transformation from overwhelming defeat by South Africa to pushing the All Blacks hard for their victory come about? My role in it was minimal, in a direct sense. I might have a word here or there, or perhaps sit down with one of the guys for an hour or so if necessary and have a couple of beers with him. It's the sort of involvement whereby you have to make people believe in themselves, to make them think that if they really want something to happen it will happen. The selectors got it right and that was a vital factor. They reacted well to the autumn defeats and picked the on-form men – guys like Damian Cronin and Dave Hilton, for example – for the Canada match. Slowly we began to gel. By the time we had finished the Five Nations we were a

team. At international level that is so important. It may seem an obvious truth, but you can't play well if you're not all in it together. If Scotland ever became complacent in the build-up to any match then I don't think that we would perform half as well as we have been doing. We may not be the greatest rugby players in the world, but there is a confidence and self-belief, a sense of team spirit, in this squad which few other countries were able to match in the World Cup.

We did well in our opening pool games against the Ivory Coast and Tonga in that we held our shape and played to our strengths when it would have been so easy to lose concentration once we were a few points up. I was obviously pretty pleased with my own form – 44 points is not a bad return for one match, no matter who the opposition are.

It was always going to be the case that France would be a crunch game. My savage disappointment at losing to them had nothing whatsoever to do with the fact that defeat meant we had to face the All Blacks rather than Ireland in the quarter-final. I was desperately unhappy in the aftermath of the French match simply because we had lost a game we should have won. I would have been delighted to have faced the All Blacks regardless of the outcome against France. If you come to a World Cup, you have got to sincerely want to face any side in the competition and be confident of beating them. We played well against France, but just did not manage to close the game right down when it mattered most.

The prospect of meeting the All Blacks, who had been impressive in their pool games, did not worry me in the slightest. I'd played them over a dozen times and, although I'd never beaten them with Scotland, I had known victory against them with the British Lions. Looking back, I felt we would have won the series in 1993 if only we'd had a bit more self-belief. The Blacks were no supermen, that was for sure, and that was the message I was putting across to the boys during the week building up to our quarter-final in Pretoria.

I'd received a kick in the lower back against France so

I had not been able to train fully. A lot of our talk in that time focused on how we might stop Jonah Lomu. He had made some impact during the pool matches and it would have been madness not to have addressed the issue. As it was, we decided that we would grab and fall with him rather than try to knock him back in his stride. In the end the theory was much easier than the practice.

We were disappointed in the scores we gave away against the Blacks. We'd had a good opening and then decided to run a penalty under the posts towards the end of the first half when we would have been better advised to kick the goal and take the three points. That would have given us a lead just before half-time, which would have made a psychological difference. Then came the big blow. New Zealand hit us twice for tries in the opening minutes of the second half, and we were dead and buried.

We stuck at it, but it was only then a matter of finishing with some pride. That we did with the tries we scored.

For me it was some way to finish. Of course, I would have preferred to have ended on a winning note, but in sport you simply can't write the script. The Scottish support in Pretoria was fantastic and it gave us the best possible send-off. It was an emotional day, that's for sure. The whole World Cup was a marvellously successful event, and for people to still be coming up and congratulating me two weeks after Scotland had been knocked out of the tournament showed what a great rugby country South Africa is. It was a huge compliment to me. For me the World Cup and my career certainly didn't finish on a sad note. **)**

As Scotland made their exit from the World Cup, their retiring captain, Gavin Hastings, former British Lions captain, was described by New Zealand skipper Sean Fitzpatrick as the best full-back in world rugby.

"Take me to the Hilton."

The truck driver laughed. His first words had been "G'day, mate – anything I can do?" But hitching a lift was a bit impractical. Within minutes, we'd called for help on the truck's impressive radio, and let the Hilton know I'd be late.

Seeing his friendly face reminded me how much I was looking forward to meeting the Hilton people again; they always made me feel particularly welcome. He climbed into his cab. "Hilton, eh?" Wanna change places?"

I thought about the cold beers and cool sheets waiting for me. "No chance," I said, waving him on his way. "But thanks."

HILTON
Where you can be your *self* again.

The Durban Semi-final
France so close to glory in Durban downpour
Clem Thomas

Who was it who said it never rains in Durban, South Africa's principal sunshine resort, in May or June? It was so torrentially wet for the semi-final, with 7ins of rain in 24 hours, that the players scarcely needed a shower afterwards. The old saying that it never rains but it pours was never better exemplified: aircraft bringing in fans from all parts of the Republic were forced to circle for up to an hour before landing. Indeed, this was a game which should never have been played. In any other circumstances, any sensible authority or the referee would have called it off.

There was no doubt that the game ought to have been postponed until the next day, but the expediency of the World Cup made the officials lose their objectivity. Their only consideration should have been whether a game of such importance as a World Cup semi-final should have

The torrential downpour flooded the Durban pitch and delayed the start of the first semi-final.

The Natal authorities managed to find a regiment of charladies. Here they are seen sweeping the water off the pitch.

Fabien Galthié, the French scrum-half, is stopped just short of the line. South Africa's James Small and Hennie le Roux look on.

been turned into what was a virtually a lottery.

Regardless of the monsoon conditions, the Natal authorities found a regiment of black charladies from heaven knows where to sweep some of the standing water off the pitch. In spite of lightning and the black gloom of impending thunderclouds, the game was allowed to kick off an hour and a half late. There were also problems behind the scenes, when the Springboks announced a change in their jersey numbering and introduced a new set of jerseys. The match director, John Jeavons-Fellows, a Rugby Union committee member and a member of the International Board, insisted that that they should change back into their original strip. Morné du Plessis, the Springbok manager, said that the jerseys had left the stadium in the team van with the baggage master. Louis Luyt then added his considerable weight to the proceedings, only to be told by Jeavons-Fellows that the match was due to start in seven minutes and that, unless

they played in their original strip, then, according to the rules of the tournament, they would forfeit the game. The jerseys were quickly produced.

What the South African camp had not perhaps fully realised was that had the game been abandoned at any point once it had started, if at that stage there was no score or the teams were level and South Africa had not scored a try, then the Springboks would have forfeited the match. The World Cup rules clearly stated that in the event of a draw in such circumstances the team with the least number of players sent off in the tournament would be deemed to have won. Having had James Dalton sent off against Canada, they were extremely vulnerable.

While there was no rain when the match finally kicked off, the heavens opened again within ten minutes. Derek Bevan, the referee, allowed it to continue. In such awful conditions the game became a complete farce, the French beating into the wind in the first half and the Springboks

*Pieter du Randt, the South African prop
forward, drives menacingly towards the French
line moments before the game's first try.*

forced to weather the storm – and what a storm it was – as France counter-attacked in the second period. The French, who had never led throughout the match, launched challenges which had South Africa reeling and clinging desperately to a narrow lead. As Kitch Christie, the Springbok coach, said afterwards, 'It was a bunfight out there and South Africa were fortunate to be holding the bun at the last.' In truth France had reason to be aggrieved, for the television analysis of the game by the neutral Australians showed that almost every decision went against them, and when the second of three successive rucks on the Springbok line in the closing couple of minutes was dropped as it was going forward, there was the strongest possible case for a penalty try to be awarded, particularly as the French went for it and threw three of their backs into the shove.

There had been considerable selectorial activity in both camps before the game. Kitch Christie astounded us

by picking the splendid Mark Andrews, the giant lock who has emerged as one of the finest line-out jumpers in the game, at No. 8. Most of South Africa, too, was stunned by the selection, as Andrews had not played in that position since he was at school. In the event the decision proved to be a success and Kitch Christie continued to walk on water. Meanwhile, Pierre Berbizier, the French coach, who had not lost a game in the southern hemisphere since he took over in 1992, dropped his scrum-half, Aubin Hueber, who had helped to secure the quarter-final win over Ireland, and replaced him with the controversial Fabien Galthié. Galthié, if you remember, was one of the architects of the defeat of France in that notorious quarter-final against England in Paris in the 1991 World Cup, when time and again he took wrong options.

Hueber responded with a virulent attack on Berbizier in the French press, accusing him of having favourites. Apparently, the half-backs had had a run-in during

Mark Andrews, considered by many as a controversial choice at No. 8 for South Africa, celebrates his side's first try.

Abdel Benazzi bulldozes into the South African defence. In the final minutes, he came within inches of winning the game for France.

training, when Hueber had rowed with the fly-half, Christophe Deylaud. Berbizier admitted that the change had little to do with rugby; Galthié, he explained, was in a better frame of mind. It was ever thus with the French, among whom personality clashes and temperament play a big part in events. Indeed, there was some talk that France lacked motivation and purpose, and it was certainly true that there were some considerable differences between players and that Berbizier was not in complete control of his squad. In the end, the French coach must have pondered on whether he ought to have listened to Hueber's criticism of the Toulouse fly-half, who had his second poor game in succession. His kicking was so weak that it probably cost them the match.

Even though the pitch was virtually an unplayable swamp, the very fact that this was a semi-final was enough to make the game hugely absorbing, in spite of the water trickling down your neck and soaking you to the skin. It

was a credit to both sides that they managed, somehow, to play some coherent rugby in the conditions. South Africa, playing with a strong wind at at their backs, acquired a 10–6 lead in the first half. Joel Stransky scored a penalty goal in the second minute after Andrews won a ball at the front of a line-out which set up a drive from which France were penalised. Then, more crucially, after 27 minutes came a try, by their outstanding flanker, Ruben Kruger. After a charged-down kick, Joost van der Westhuizen made a break from the ensuing line-out for François Pienaar and Kobus Wiese to drive on. Kruger proved how adept he is by snatching the ball to be driven over the line. Stransky converted. It seemed that France were now dead and buried, but some poor Springbok discipline and backchat to the referee saw Thierry Lacroix resurrect them with two timely penalty goals.

In the second half, the French began to fight back in earnest and Pienaar and the South African forwards

André Joubert clears the ball under immense pressure from Philippe Sella and Thierry Lacroix. The South African full-back was playing the game with a broken hand.

*Fabien Galthié desperately tries to free the ball
from the maul.*

started to look brittle as the formidable French pack, with Laurent Cabannes and Abdelatif Benazzi in stupendous form, proceeded to give them a hard time. The Springboks now repulsed wave after wave of French attack but the only further scores came from the respective boots of Stransky and Lacroix, who cancelled each other out with three penalties apiece.

With four minutes to go to full time, the game built up to a colossal climax during which the French threw every last ounce of energy into their bid for what might have been a great victory. The Springboks visibly wilted before the savagery of the attack, which in the end came to nothing. André Joubert, one of the best players in the tournament, uncharacteristically dropped a high ball, one of the few hoisted by Deylaud, who had been tactically negligent in this regard. Benazzi collected it and stormed his way to within inches of scoring. The French, now confident in their forward supremacy,

elected to go for a pushover try from three successive scrums on the Springbok line. It was agony for friend and foe alike to watch, as both the first and second scrums collapsed. The second in particular, when France threw 11 men into the scrum, seemed to scream penalty try. The referee, however, deemed otherwise. The French now desperately ran their last piece of possession. Le Roux and Stransky put in a last-ditch tackle on Lacroix which sent South Africa into the dream final against New Zealand and on the path to the greatest glory in their history.

Berbizier was generous in defeat and declined to criticise the referee. He merely said, 'If a penalty try was on in the last minute, it was up to Bevan to give it.' The recriminations were to come a couple of days later. The South African captain, François Pienaar was overjoyed. 'The last five minutes were heart-stopping,' he said. And so they were.

What they said . . .

François Pienaar: 'I suppose it was not an attractive game, but we won – that's what counts…. We will only know tomorrow what we feel to be in the final. We can't put it into words. It is our first appearance in the World Cup and we are in the final – it is wonderful.'

Pierre Berbizier: 'The players played their hearts out – thanks to South Africa, who helped us to have a good game. I am proud of my team. To lose in the semi-final is hard…. I think Bevan reffed well. If a penalty try was on in the last minute it was up to him to give it. He is the best in the world.'

Kitch Christie: 'We will look at the videos to plan for New Zealand. They are the best and we will have to play well. We will look carefully at where our mistakes were: in the line-outs, rucks or wherever.'

French coach
Pierre Berbizier.

South Africa's coach Kitch Christie (left) and manager Morné du Plessis.

succeed where competition is fierce

THE **PILKINGTON** CUP

In highly competitive international markets, Pilkington stays ahead manufacturing and marketing flat and safety glass products in over 20 countries around the globe.

PILKINGTON

SPONSORS OF THE RFU CLUB KNOCKOUT COMPETITIONS

The Cape Town Semi-final

All over for England in a matter of minutes
Bill McLaren

One game in particular generated massive interest among rugby folk everywhere and not least among the huge numbers of English and New Zealand supporters who packed the hotels and bars of South Africa, proclaiming to all and sundry the merits of their World Cup squads before the Cape Town semi-final. New Zealand versus England conjured up magical visions of an earth-shattering confrontation between the number three and number two seeds. Could England sink a second southern hemisphere heavyweight as they had done on the same Newlands ground a week previously? Then they had beaten the reigning world champions, Australia, with Rob Andrew's priceless late dropped goal. Now they were required to peak again to take on the most feared Rugby Union nation in the world, who had scored 35 tries in their opening four games and who, at times, had appeared

Jonah Lomu brushes off Tony Underwood. It was a torrid game for the England wing, as Lomu went on to score four tries.

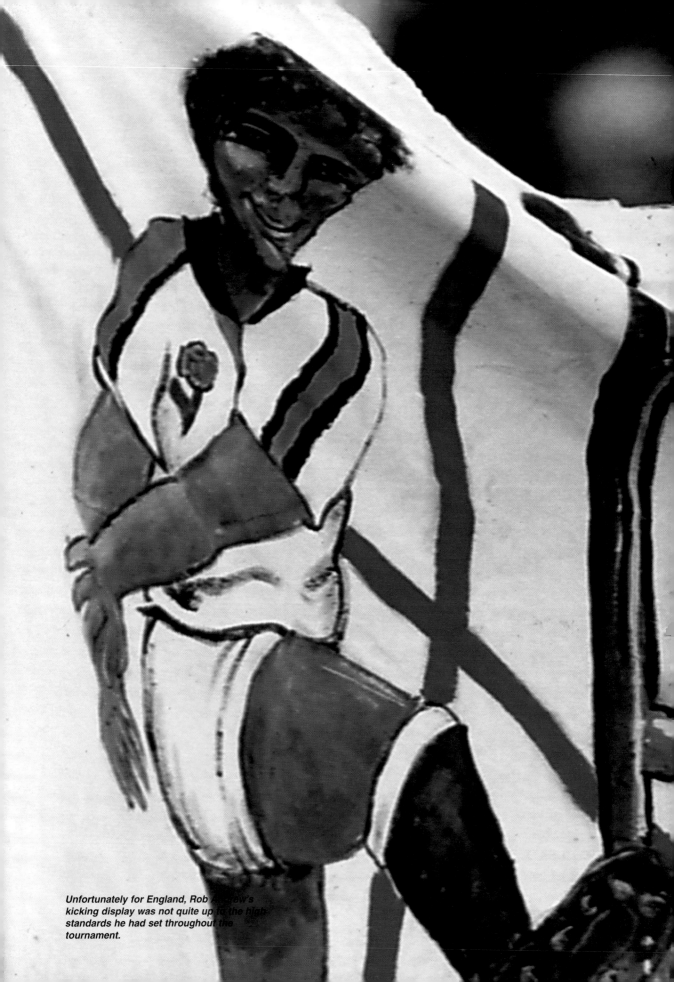

Unfortunately for England, Rob Andrew's kicking display was not quite up to the high standards he had set throughout the tournament.

Martin Johnson, policed by Zinzan Brooke, tries to pressurise the New Zealand defence.

Those who had cited Lomu's defensive weaknesses were silenced after this match. Try as he might, Tony Underwood could not outpace the New Zealand giant.

simply awesome. All the talk was of how England's big line-out would starve the All Blacks of essential fodder; of how the massive English pack would exert control over the proceedings; of how Rob Andrew would expose, with his educated boot, the defensive deficiencies of Jonah Lomu; of how Andrew would kick all the goals in a glorious English victory.

New Zealand, for their part, simply sought to create a fertile platform from which their very quick hands, with openside flanker Josh Kronfeld as their ally, would spin the ball in the manner that had so discomfited the gallant Scots. They also had one priority: to get the ball to Lomu in space.

The match exceeded expectations. It was ablaze with movement, with Herculean forward exchanges, with shuddering tackles aimed at knocking opponents backwards but which, in general, were fair, and with some spectacular handling which gave the capacity crowd a thoroughly entertaining afternoon. It was a personal triumph for Lomu. He scored four of New Zealand's six tries with thunderous runs in which he left opponents grasping thin air. He crashed through tackles like an earth-mover and demonstrated that he is singularly athletic, highly skilled and possesses an edge of acceleratory pace that catches opponents by surprise. As for exposing his defensive vulnerability, it is true that Will Carling scored one of his two tries down in Lomu's left-hand corner, but the giant wing was not at fault there. Moreover, once he got back to effect a lengthy saving clearance (even if it suggested that he has only one kicking foot, the left), a

The New Zealand forwards create a perfect platform for Graeme Bachop to release his backs.

popular belief before the game that Tony Underwood would be England's key man foundered on Lomu's ability not only to match the younger Underwood for pace, but to grab him by the neck and throw him into touch for all the world like an Olympic hammer-thrower. The mouth watered at the thought of Lomu and South Africa's James Small locking horns in the final.

That the All Blacks were focused and alert to the main chance was shown by the manner in which they caught England cold at the beginning of each half. New Zealand coach Laurie Mains said at the post-match press conference that they had planned for the All Blacks to take the initiative right from the start. The 22-year-old fly-half, Andrew Mehrtens, took the kick-off for which Sean Fitzpatrick had opted on winning the toss, but instead of

the orthodox kick to his forwards, he put in a delicate little chip shot, like a wedge at golf, to the blind side and just over the 10 metres. It was a sucker punch which caught out England. Within seconds of that crafty start New Zealand had created a bridgehead from which Lomu crashed past three tackles for the opening try less than three minutes into the match. Two minutes later the All Blacks made a clear declaration of intent when, from inside their own 22, Walter Little and Glen Osborne counter-attacked in a blaze of black. Just when the move seemed stillborn, Kronfeld appeared like an express train to crash over for Mehrtens to convert. When the fly-half added a penalty goal New Zealand were 15 points up in 11 minutes and playing a scintillating brand of rugby that England just could not match. It was 25–3 at half-time

England lock Martin Johnson beats
Robin Brooke to the ball.

And then the dream was over...Rob Andrew
consoles the England captain as he tries to
come to terms with defeat.

The England captain crosses the line to score one of his two tries, and in doing so adds some respectability to the scoreline.

from Mehrtens' conversion of Lomu's second try and a dropped goal from Zinzan Brooke which underlined my own view that he is the most skilled and tactically aware forward in the world game. He gathered a loose ball some 40 metres out and smacked over a cracking goal that put the icing on an already very rich New Zealand cake.

Perhaps it was no coincidence that when Zinzan Brooke departed with an ankle twist the All Black effort lost its momentum – but not before Lomu and Graeme Bachop, who had a magnificent match, had added tries of brilliant creation and skilled execution. Bachop's was a gem. A scrummage pick-up enabled him to threaten enough to disrupt the set-piece defence, whereupon he supported a thrilling breakout by Osborne and Jeff Wilson before sailing home to take the score to 35–3 after 51 minutes.

To their credit, England kept their heads high and, inspired by Dewi Morris, who recovered from a shaky start, they staged an admirable rally and a see-saw spectacular to ring down the curtain with two tries each for Will Carling (his tenth and 11th) and Rory Underwood, who raised his record tally to 47. Only David Campese of Australia has scored more international tries (63). Rob Andrew, who badly hooked his first two penalty attempts, did succeed with three conversions and one penalty for an all-in total in major internationals of 388. Yet each time England threatened serious revival the All Blacks countered to effect. They were rewarded by Lomu's fourth try, from a huge Mehrtens spin pass, converted by Mehrtens, and then a dropped goal for the talented fly-half. It brought his tally to 15 points in the

match and 75 from four games.

The final score after a contest of rare movement and mighty endeavour was 45–29, and the All Blacks emerged as even firmer favourites to win the World Cup for the second time.

England may have reflected on what they might have achieved had they not turned so much of their ball back to their loose forwards, had they not punted so much, had they spun the ball more. It was only in desperation, at 35–3 adrift, that they showed how lethal their backs could be when given their heads. Carling set a splendid example in never-say-die spirit and there were several vintage glimpses of the Jeremy Guscott magic with its crucial element of a searing change in pace.

Yet the feeling remained that the All Blacks had attained a higher level of team play, of reactive speed and of commitment to the tackle which set them apart. They were thoroughly deserving qualifiers for the World Cup final in which they were to clash with their traditional heavyweight rivals, the Springboks. It was to be their 39th meeting. New Zealand had 16 wins, South Africa 20 and two games had been drawn. A juicy prospect indeed.

A distraught Will Carling leaves the pitch at the end of the game.

What they said . . .

Sean Fitzpatrick: 'We wanted to be in the final, not the play-offs. We wanted to win desperately. The 1993 loss against England was a motivating factor, but, as I say, we wanted to play in the final. We didn't read the papers this week, as we didn't need the motivation from the press. It came from within. A good start was important and that first try helped us a lot. It was a nail in their coffin.'

Brian Lochore: 'The Springboks will be extremely hard to beat on Saturday as they will have the whole country behind them now. It is great for South Africa but bad for us. We are used to having our backs to the wall and will do our best to beat South Africa.'

Will Carling: 'They made an unbelievable start. I have never endured anything like it. Lomu is a freak, an incredible athlete. The sooner he goes away the better. We could have buckled even more, but we came back with some tries and we can be proud of that. Nobody is blaming Tony Underwood. We win as a team and we lose as a team.'

Jack Rowell: 'Lomu is a phenomenon. He plays a different game. We had enough chances to have scored 12 or 15 points by half-time, and in the end the margin was 16 points. New Zealand have allied traditional New Zealand forward strength with exciting runners in the backs and are playing a totally different game.'

Mike Catt: 'Lomu just ran straight over me. I didn't know before the match just how big he was. They are a class outfit, but every ball bounced their way.'

All Black manager Brian Lochore with former coach Colin Meads.

The two captains come face to face. Will Carling and Sean Fitzpatrick during the semi-final.

Rob Andrew

❛ The process is far from finished: that can be the only message to draw from our semi-final defeat by New Zealand. We knew that whatever happened in the match, we were not the complete item. We'd come a long way since we first met up in August for a training camp. Then the senior players set about convincing the new ones that we could genuinely win the competition. You don't find confidence overnight, and you can't contrive it. In 1991, Will Carling, Brian Moore, myself and others had been content just to get to the final. That sort of halfway attitude cost us dear in the end. The Aussies beat us because they wanted it more.

This time around we were determined not to make the same mistake. Of course, in the end we lost, but I don't believe that it was from a lack of application. A lot of sweat was expended through the year, what with the matches themselves and, during the autumn, the fortnightly meets at Marlow. Those gatherings were essential if we were to foster the spirit which had taken us so far in 1991. That team had been through a lot together.

By the time the Five Nations finished, this current squad had accumulated some experience. The hefty wins over Romania and Canada, plus the control and poise of our success in Dublin and victories over France and against Wales in Cardiff, are not a bad return. And then came the Grand Slam over Scotland. We spluttered a bit in that match, but given the claustrophobia of the tournament, and the variable conditions, we were very happy indeed as we set off for South Africa.

Where did it go wrong? We certainly did not pick up from where we left off. Our pool games were all very tough, which we knew they would be, but even so, we thought that we would fare better than we did. Perhaps deep, deep down we did have our eyes on the quarter-final. If we did, we certainly paid the price, for those pool games were all bruising affairs. The match against Argentina was desperately disappointing. Our forwards were devastated afterwards because they had been thoroughly outplayed and they knew it. We hung in there, though, and with a win under our belts we fully expected to bounce back against Italy. Again, it didn't materialise. The bang we had expected to provide in the tournament was a bit of damp squib at this point. At least our match against Western Samoa got us in the groove. It was our best performance of the pool round by some distance. The fact that it was the non-front-line players who provided it gave the whole squad a boost. It was great to see guys like Damian Hopley and John Mallett get a cap; it was also good for morale. Their good showing also put pressure on the established players for their places.

Now that we were through to the quarter-final and a reunion with Australia, whom we'd last met back in the 1991 final, we knew we had to be spot-on or we'd be on the plane home. Even if you're struggling there is nothing too radical that you can do to get things on the move. International rugby is fairly straightforward and simple in that you have to get the basics right and then work from there. If the set-piece possession is scrappy, the backs have no targets to hit. You simply have to go forward, so if the pack isn't firing then your job is extremely difficult. In that build-up week we just plugged away at our usual routines. We were not searching for the impossible, because we'd played some decent stuff in the course of the season and we knew that it would come again.

Despite the rocky beginning to the competition our confidence was quite good. We'd beaten both South Africa and New Zealand in the preceding 18 months and knew therefore that we were capable of getting past anyone. There were nerves in the camp, though, because we knew that this was the moment when the World Cup really kicked off. Ours was the biggest of the quarter-finals and so everything came into sharp focus. It wasn't hard to get the players to concentrate in the team meetings that week. People often wonder how you cope with the pressure of the big games. In fact it's usually easier to prepare for them than it is for a run-of-the-mill match. Your mind just hones in on every last detail because you know that if you don't get it right, you're finished.

And so to Australia. What a great start we had! The crowd was right behind us, so much so that it was almost like Twickenham. We overwhelmed the Aussies in that opening period and might have scored more often than we did. The try was just an instinctive decision. I was on to the loose ball and we were away. Jerry reacted well outside me and Tony did brilliantly to finish off. We ought not have given away a ten-point lead, but we did. The second half was not that spectacular, but boy, was it tense. This was real pressure, and even I would admit that I thought we'd run out of time. It would have been very easy, with six minutes remaining and trailing by three points, to have thrown in the towel. This is when those tough days in Paris and Dublin pay off. You learn a lot about yourselves as a team in those situations.

As it turned out, the opportunity did come our way. There was a huge amount of coverage of my winning drop-kick, but let me tell you that the really difficult kick was not that one but the equalising penalty. I was far more pleased about knocking that one over than I was the drop-kick. If I'd missed the penalty we would have been out. The drop-kick was do or die. I'd never, ever hit one like that. I watched it all the way just in case. I knew, though, that I'd hit it sweetly.

What a fall-out there was from that match! The whole place just erupted. Yet a week can make a big difference. We approached the All Blacks in the same way as we had the Aussies – we knew we had the beating of them. Perhaps, though, we underestimated their ferocity, I just don't know. We were certainly fazed by what happened and we were out of it after ten minutes. The mood afterwards was one of complete bewilderment rather than devastation. This was a huge smack in the mouth and a big blow for a side which still considers itself to be up there with the best. It's almost as if the New Zealand match was a bad dream. I hope I wake up soon. **'**

At times, Rob Andrew kept England's World Cup dreams alive. His last-minute dropped goal against Australia will go down in history as one of the greatest kicks of all time. But even he could do nothing to stop the All Black machine.

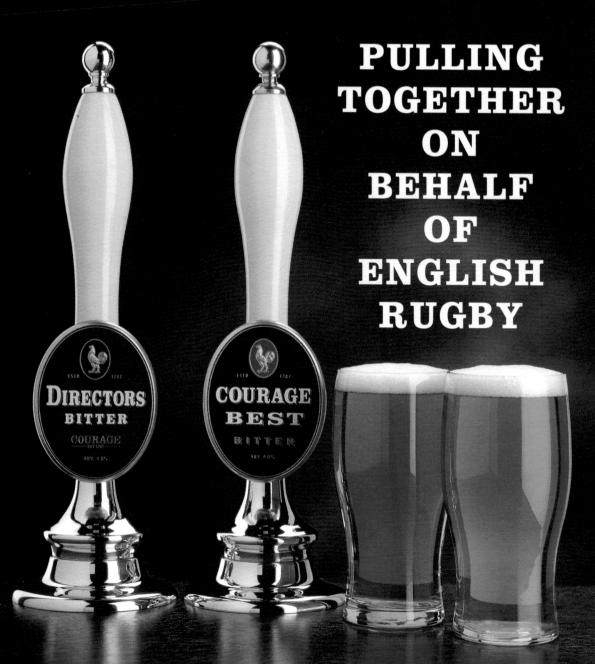

PULLING TOGETHER ON BEHALF OF ENGLISH RUGBY

Proud Sponsors of
The Courage Clubs Championship
and the England Squad

The 3rd/4th Play-off
The game no one wanted
Mick Cleary

It was the game that no one wanted. The third-fourth-place play-off is a difficult match in any competition, and perhaps it will always be a redundant affair. Moreover, here both teams had lost their semi-finals in traumatic fashion and so were scarcely in any fit mental state to get back out there just a few days later to give a meaningful performance.

France had been involved in the monsoon match in Durban which, at one point, looked as if it would be postponed. It was played, of course, in atrocious conditions, and France were denied at the death only by three centimetres when a charge by Benazzi was held just short of the South African try-line. England got nowhere near as close. Their defeat by New Zealand was all the harder to recover from simply because they had been humiliated. The scoreboard might tell you that they got within 16 points of the All Blacks; those who were there will tell you that they were not within a country mile of them.

'It's so hard to get up for the game,' said England prop Victor Ubogu. 'This will be a test of our resolve,' agreed Rob Andrew. Across town in Pretoria, the French were trying to put a braver face on it. 'We are going to make pleasure on the pitch,' said Philippe Sella. His fly-half and old sparring partner in the centre, Franck Mesnel, restored to the colours, was also in upbeat mood. 'We are going to run it,' he said.

The game itself belied their confidence, and afterwards both teams admitted that it was a virtual impossiblity to prepare players for such a match. Why on earth a knock-out competition should deem it worthwhile to know who finishes third, when none of the other lesser placings need to be determined, is an anomaly which has yet to be addressed. This time around the organisers did try to apend some sort of significance to the match by stating that it would serve as a qualifying game for the World Cup in 1999. The winner would go through automatically; the loser would have to battle it out in Spain, Portugal or some other entirely, with all due respect, ridiculous venue. There is such a gulf in standards already that to pit some worthy second-string country

Abdelatif Benazzi, the impressive French flanker, seizes the loose ball.

Jeremy Guscott collects his thoughts during what turned out to be a particularly disappointing game for England.

against one of the big guns runs the risk of exposing the underdog to mockery and the possible regression of their game. If there were any real merit in qualification, then this game ought to have been played in proper circumstances.

Sean Fitzpatrick had told the England camp on the previous Sunday that they would find it difficult. They made it no easier for themselves by insisting on sticking with the tried and trusted players. All bar one that is – Tony Underwood was dropped (officially he was 'rested', but such euphemisms serve only to highlight the true situation) after his ordeal by Lomu. Underwood was obviously shattered by the experience, but so were several others. 'We still consider Tony to be the best right wing in the country,' said Jack Rowell. If that were really the case, he should have been allowed to get back on his bike after his horrible accident and learn to ride again. If not, then he should not have been singled out. If ever a game cried out for the fresh lungs and sharp appetites of the dirt-trackers, it was this one. The likes of Graham Rowntree, John Mallett and Damian Hopley, who had been glorified tackle-bags for the best part of six weeks, would have done England proud. They had shown as much in the battle of Port Elizabeth (the match in which

Tim Rodber was sent off) the previous year. Rowell, though, preferred to stick with those he knew. 'It's a one-off and there's been no time to prepare,' said the England manager. The only other change saw Steve Ojomoh come in for the injured Dean Richards.

France made three changes, bringing in Mesnel for Deylaud, Benezech for Armary at prop and, perhaps the most popular decision of the whole of the tournament among the French, awarding a first cap at No. 8 to 34-year-old Albert Cigagna of Toulouse, long considered to be the best player never to have won international honours. Pierre Berbizier also tried to make the right noises about the match in prospect.

'Like England, we want to finish on the best possible note,' he said. 'We know their sense of pride and that they are capable of lifting their game after defeat.'

Berbizier was wrong. England never looked remotely like being able to lift their game. In front of a larger than expected crowd of 44,000 at Loftus Versfeld, they started flat and finished flat. It was not so much that their legs were shot to bits, for that was entirely understandable. They were pushed around in the scrummage and knocked about in the line-outs. There was no surprise in that, for they had had a day's less recuperation than the

Rory Underwood tries to shrug off the challenge of the recalled French fly-half Franck Mesnel.

Martin Johnson, with the support of Jason Leonard and Victor Ubogu, beats Laurent Benezech of France.

Hastings' record tally for the tournament. Good tackling, particularly by Dewi Morris, in his last match for England, on Cabannes and by Ojomoh on Sadourny helped keep the England try-line intact. Saint-André was pulled down just short on one occasion.

Will Carling obviously dished out a few choice words at half-time, because England came out with more bite to their play in the second half, so much so that Ben Clarke, who had a great tournament, was warned for stamping in the very first minute. Lacroix kicked the penalty. It was not boots and bullets that England needed, just a few movements of pace and imagination across the back line. Instead they relied on predictable means to accumulate points, Andrew's boot bringing them level in the eighth minute of the half when Benazzi was penalised for scrabbling on the deck with his hands.

Lacroix, though, nudged his side back in front six minutes later. By now France were beginning to flow. Cabannes, Sella and Ntamack were all showing. The inevitable happened in the 59th minute. After one long, sweeping movement took France downfield, Hunter's tackle finally halted the charge just a few metres from the

Ben Clarke's aggressive charge is thwarted by Jean-Michel Gonzalez.

French and a far harder World Cup programme than their opponents to boot. What made their performance so inexcusable, though, was not these lapses. Rather it was their attitude of once again playing a kick-and-chase game when the occasion cried out for a team to make light of a meaningless (easy to say, I know, from the sanctuary of the press box) match and to try to carve openings by running. Even if one ignores the mind-numbing tedium of the kick-and-chase tactic and its aesthetic limitations, there was simply no purchase in it, either. Every time England kicked high they lost possession. Full-backs like Jean-Luc Sadourny are now, in the style of Aussie Rules footballers, so adept at leaping to take the high ball that the percentage return must be much lower than it was. But England persisted and with the strategy lost the match as well as many friends.

The half-time score of 3–3 told its own sterile story. Rob Andrew knocked over a penalty in the 26th minute from 40 metres after barging in the line-out while Thierry Lacroix replied with almost the last kick of the half for France, which took him to 106 points and so past Gavin

Laurent Cabannes penetrates a gap in England's defence. The French forward had one of his best games of the World Cup.

England line. But Merle won the line-out and the French forwards gathered round and drove Roumat over the line. Lacroix hit the post with the conversion.

From the restart France infringed and Andrew put three more points on the board. These were paltry times for England: the scrum was under immense pressure and if it hadn't been for the galvanising presence and play of both Morris and Clarke, they might have been swept away. France were looking to set up their outside runners at every turn and it was no surprise or injustice when Ntamack was put away down the blind side a minute from time. The burly, magnetic winger cut inside two tacklers on his way to the try-line.

'We wanted desperately to perform,' said Will Carling afterwards. 'That we didn't was due to mental reasons. There was a challenge there for us tonight and we didn't respond.' England manager Jack Rowell simply pointed out the magnitude of the experience his players had gone through in the preceding 11 days. 'To play Australia, New Zealand and France within such a short space of time is asking a lot,' said Rowell. 'We hit a brick wall last Sunday against the All Blacks, which is when our World Cup effectively ended. I think you saw that tonight.'

Will Carling leaves the pitch to contemplate England's second successive defeat.

A crunching tackle for Will Carling as he tries to break through French lines.

What they said . . .

Will Carling: 'It was not a lack of skill, but we came here to win the World Cup and, having had that prize taken away from us, found it hard to pick ourselves up. We desperately wanted to win to keep our record against France going and so that we could return home on a winning note. Now we have lost two consecutive Tests for the first time since 1991. It is not something we will shrug off.'

Jack Rowell: 'We got to the last four, and one year ago I did not think we could manage that, because either Australia or South Africa would stand in our way at the quarter-final stage. Part of today's result is explained by the fact that we ran into a brick wall against the All Blacks, and any team needs a long time to recover from the experience of being on the wrong end of a hammering by New Zealand. Basically, I guess that the players did not want to play this game.'

Philippe Saint-André: 'Only Sella and Mesnel of my team have had the delight of beating England, so it was gratifying for the younger generation. I have always lost against Will Carling, so I took special pleasure in shaking hands with him with a smile on my face while he stared at the grass.'

Pierre Berbizier: 'It was certainly difficult preparing a team for a match so soon after the dejection of losing a semi-final, but we were more highly motivated. Now that we have overcome England after seven years and have qualified automatically for the next World Cup, we can take our summer holidays relaxed and assured.'

Philippe Saint-André takes a break during the play-off against England.

IT WAS WORTH THE WAIT.

The final whistle has blown. The players have left the field. The pitch bears the scars of the sporting giants who have stormed down it on their way to victory or defeat. Now, only the memories remain. And the memories of thousands of avid rugby fans visiting our beautiful land to watch their heroes do battle under an African sky. Lured here by their love of the sport. Brought here by South African Airways.

The Final

A nation on a knife edge
Tony O'Reilly

It is Saturday 24 June and the headline in the Johannesburg *Star* reads, 'a nation on a knife edge', which says it all.

There is an air of indescribable excitement as we drive through the crystalline noon light to Ellis Park, and my mind's eye flashes back to 40 years before, to what turned out to be one of the epic encounters in rugby history. Then, before 105,000 people, the British Lions, reduced to only 14 men after the first 11 minutes (there were no replacements in those days), defeated South Africa as Jack van der Schyff mysteriously missed an easy final conversion which would have made it 24–23 to the Springboks. I remember one of my fellow Lions asking me what I was thinking at the time of that fateful kick. I replied: 'I was in direct communication with the Vatican.'

Casting my mind back to those days, with all the affection and romance that distance lends, I still think that it was not remotely as exciting as what is about to happen at Ellis Park this afternoon, and what a different Ellis Park it is. The new stadium is much more comfortable, but in a sense much smaller, than that which greeted 105,000 rugby worshippers 40 years ago. My impression of that game was of the brilliance and electric movements of Clifford Isaac Morgan, our great star. When he rounded Basie van Wyk for a try, it was an act of revenge for a torrid afternoon he had spent four years previously during the Springboks' triumphant 1951 tour of the British Isles. On that long, bleak afternoon, as Cliff recounted it, Hennie Müller, Stephen Fry and Basie van Wyk had almost hunted him off the rugby field. That glittering knife-like thrust under the posts that took us into the lead remains the great recollection of my life in rugby football. I was all of 19 at the time and to me the day had a special excitement, but in a way more remembered in the afterglow than at the time.

Three months later, after a series punctuated by brilliance, generosity and the discovery of great stars of the future such as Tom van Vollenhoven, Dan Retief, Wilf Rosenberg and Roy Dryburgh, we ended the series at 2–2 on a sunlit afternoon in Port Elizabeth. The warmth of my memories of that team and that series – and indeed, of so many of my South African friends whom I have met in the last few weeks – has prompted a certain confusion in my mind, for in a sense it was the spirit of gaiety and unbounded enthusiasm, a sort of Corinthian ideal, that was celebrated in that eventful summer of 1955. I wonder if all this will now be put at risk if the game, as appears inevitable, goes nakedly professional.

The answer is possibly academic, since it has already been given by the southern hemisphere unions, and certainly seems to meet with the tacit approval of most of the players, on whom extraordinary demands are placed nowadays. However, many great rugby players have learned nothing other than rugby and have acquired few of the skills required by later life, an often hapless plight, and the intensity and the obligations of the new game will make the securing of professional training ever more difficult. Yet, as all these random thoughts course through my mind as we drive towards Ellis Park, I am struck by the nature of the new rugby, of its extraordinary pulling power as a great exhibition and a national symphony. Rugby football, a recreation in my day, has become part of the gigantic world of entertainment, its customer the global consumer, its spiritual adviser satellite television.

As someone with a nodding acquaintance with the world of media, I acknowledge this with a certain sadness, marked by an understanding of a future that will be incalculably different. Rugby football is now part of showbiz, with all the consequences that flow in its train. Great sums will be paid for short periods to great stars but, as with most things in the cruel world of commerce, there will be a mountain of discards and broken hopes. How the authorities will cope with this and deal with their responsibilities to train, improve and educate could be one of the distinctive achievements of rugby football in the next decade.

These musings are quite secondary to the main thoughts of the day, which are of this great game about to unfold, a sort of climactic event in the lives of two countries. New Zealand has the new dynamic economy of the southern hemisphere, which comes as a surprise to many of us who knew the old New Zealand of the 1950s and 1960s when it was simply the farm and market garden

The clash between Jonah Lomu, the undoubted star of the World Cup, and rugged South African wing James Small, created a vast amount of interest. In the event, South Africa coped well with Lomu's awesome presence.

The decision to stage the closing ceremony before the final helped to create an electric atmosphere. Here the crowd are being entertained by dancers.

of the United Kingdom. It is now an Asian tiger, disputing leadership and growth goals with all the major economies of the Pacific regions. South Africa is the land of racial miracle. It is to be a sort of ultimate shoot-out at the OK Corral and an afternoon of extraordinary promise beckons.

As we approach the stadium the gaiety is infectious. The waving of the new flag of South Africa is wonderful, the pride of everyone in their new country clearly evident.

Last night I attended a wonderfully funny play entitled *Heel Against the Head*, in which, for the first time, I saw South Africa's new self-confidence in the extraordinary inventive good humour of the Afrikaner. It concerned two Jaapies on the way to the World Cup final in a sort of French bedroom farce. I enjoyed the play hugely, and my ultimate reflection was that a play with that sort of contagiously humorous insight into the heart of Afrikanerdom would have been impossible ten or 20 years ago. Last night a rainbow audience appreciated it to the full.

We have heard an announcement on the radio telling us that this final is the largest sporting event in the history of South Africa, and that over a billion people will see it worldwide on satellite television. Welcome to Hollywood! Last night I was talking to an Irish supporter who was commenting on the extraordinary intensity and scale of the attendances at the games here. He remarked that, back at his club in the south of Ireland, the attendances were so low that before each game they announced the crowd changes to the players.

Today's crowd is a joyful one, and happy milling faces abound. The gentleman who paints faces with the new South African flag is doing a roaring trade. The magic of Nelson Mandela is that, in a strange way, he has made South Africa proud of their achievement before the world and proud of themselves. My mind flickers back to my own country and the words of William Butler Yeats after the Civil War of 1922–4 in the south of Ireland and the division of the country into two parts. As Ireland tried to build a nation out of the ashes of the revolution, he observed: 'The Irish won, but then again they lost, because they never made friends with themselves.' I think that the miracle of the new South Africa is that all races and colours are, in an enduring way, making friends with one another.

I entered the gates of Ellis Park, where 40 years ago I played three times: against Northern Universities, when I first saw Rosenberg and Ulyate play; then Transvaal, whom we annihilated, though they had seven Springboks, and in that never-to-be forgotten Test match. It was a lucky ground for me, and I wondered how it would be today for South Africa.

I left the stadium after witnessing a titanic struggle, though even the notion of a titanic struggle is inadequate to convey what happened at Ellis Park today, for the alchemy of this extraordinary victory will help build a new South Africa, and in that sense this was not just about sport, it was about nation-building. So, as I have often said to myself, rugby football is an affair of the heart, and it was never more clearly demonstrated than in the events of today.

The most talented team was clearly New Zealand; the team which tried to play with a zest and an eye for the great green acres of open space were the All Blacks. Unfortunately, their ambition was interrupted by their execution, and time and again the pass either went to grass or not to hand.

For the first time in my life, and not without some pride, I had become a stringer, for the new *Sunday Independent*, a product of the Independent Group of South Africa, which would be publishing for the first time ever the next day. As I phoned in my copy, the sub-editor asked, 'What did you think of the South African pack? Who were the stars?' I replied, 'The South African pack deserves the ultimate benediction of anonymity, because each and every one of them played to a standard and a level of commitment unsurpassed in South African sporting history.'

Perhaps the one man who should be singled out was No. 6. No, not François Pienaar, who wore the jersey on the pitch, but President Nelson Mandela, who wore it off the field and, conspicuously, on the field as well, when he inaugurated this great sporting event before the kick-off. Behind the pack there was the generalship and extraordinary cool-headedness of Joel Stransky and Joost van der Westhuizen, who controlled his natural exuberance and his skill on the break to serve Stransky all afternoon, faithfully, with long, direct passes just beyond the reach of Kronfeld and Zinzan Brooke. Statistically, it is clear that Stransky won the game, but it is impossible to convey in the written word his enormous influence and calming presence throughout those tempestuous 100 minutes.

The Springbok backs tackled heroically, and Mulder's tackle on Lomu was a gem and a paradigm, if an unhappy one, for Lomu's future. Joubert, exuding a Gallic panache, was immense throughout the entire contest

Joost van der Westhuizen darts through a gap in the All Black defence, breaking the tackle of his opposite number, Graeme Bachop.

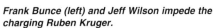

Frank Bunce (left) and Jeff Wilson impede the charging Ruben Kruger.

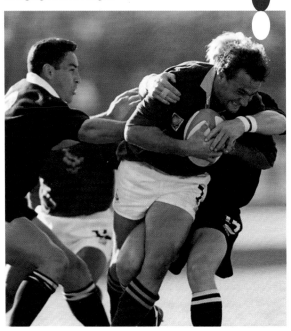

and, indeed, the tournament. The previous week, wearing a strange blue cast on his broken hand, he was definitive in Durban. Today he was simply everywhere, lofting those potent long-range kicks of his, chasing the tackle and, in particular, stopping Osborne when a try seemed on the cards. Joubert has the elegance of a croupier in a very high-class private casino and a certain war-weariness about him which was displaced in the end, when victory was clear, by wild boyish enthusiasm.

At the end of full time, both teams were deadlocked at nine points each. Neither had scored a try and at no time did either have more than a three-point lead, so the suspense was enthralling. Mehrtens could have won the match in the last minute of ordinary time, but his point-blank drop-kick from in front of the posts drifted narrowly to the right. In extra time, the All Blacks drew first blood with a penalty goal, but this was soon nullified by one from South Africa. The winning dropped goal by Stransky came seven minutes from the end of the second period of ten minutes of extra time.

In the end, as I suspected it would be, it was a

One of the few opportunities Jonah Lomu was given to run with the ball in open play. He brushes off André Joubert with the authority that he showed throughout the tournament.

question of the team effort of a gifted but limited South Africa side against the multiple talents of a young, exuberant and hugely talented New Zealand team. The ball did not run kindly for the All Blacks; passes that went to hand the preceding Sunday at Newlands today fell to ground. Bunce and Little were extremely industrious, and Lomu threatened but was quenched on so many occasions in his early strides. So,

the charm of Mehrtens, apparently fragile but immensely promising, matched by the the power of Lomu and the leggy balance of Osborne, remain the best hope for the future of New Zealand. Probably my final abiding memory of the final was the sheer athleticism of the New Zealand team, which was in almost every aspect, and certainly up front, superior to that of South Africa.

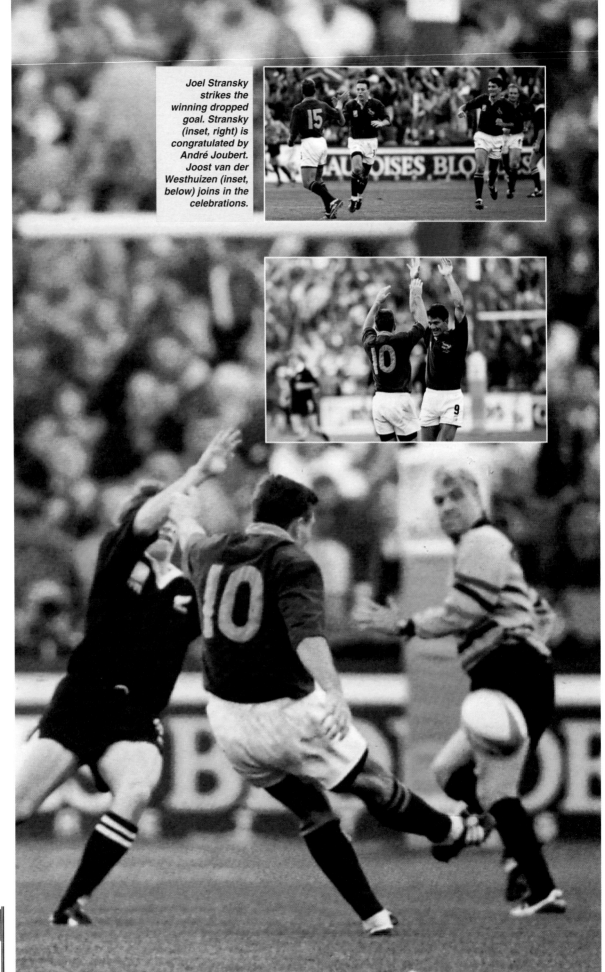

Joel Stransky strikes the winning dropped goal. Stransky (inset, right) is congratulated by André Joubert. Joost van der Westhuizen (inset, below) joins in the celebrations.

They think it's all over...it is now. The South African players joyously greet the final whistle after completing an historic victory to win the World Cup at their first attempt.

South African captain François Pienaar, watched by his President, Nelson Mandela, raises the Webb Ellis Trophy.

Yet, at the end of the day, rugby football proved again that heart, power and discipline can defeat wayward talent as strong as that of New Zealand.

I would add that the tournament was wonderfully organised and beautifully creative in its pre-match sentiments and colour.

The team which assuredly ranked with both South Africa and New Zealand were France. Unluckily defeated in Durban and clearly superior at Loftus Versfeld against England, they were, in my view, the team who could have entranced the tournament had they really got a sufficient supply of ball. In Sadourny and Ntamack they had runners of balance, elegance and pace. Perhaps the only melancholy thought of this great competition was that the public of South Africa were denied the opportunity of seeing France in full creative and innovative flight. There is no sight in world rugby like it.

What can we say of England but, sadly, that they were probably found out in South Africa? A concern expressed earlier – that a great, powerful, large, strongly committed but essentially lumbering pack would find themselves exposed on the fast grounds of the high veld – was proved to be correct; indeed, it was never more evident than in their final game against the French at Loftus. The basic notion of the England team seems to be that you can play five second-row forwards and that you can control the game by sheer physical dominance and possession. South African rugby fields are inhospitable to this idea, and England at times seemed as immobile as Wellington's squares. As I saw Cabannes and Benazzi expose the manifold weaknesses of Rodber and Clarke, I felt that England would reflect on this and perhaps, next time, include a flank forward of the pace and creativity of Neil Back.

My own country, Ireland, were spasmodic and ultimately disappointing. They had players of real class in Corkery and Geoghegan, and not a great deal in between. What they have to do is to decide what the style of Irish rugby is going to be, pick people to play accordingly, and commit to those players over extended time-frames.

The Scots, under the gallant and respected leadership of Gavin Hastings, played to their potential and look promising for the future. As I have often said, rugby is simply not a game without the Welsh and, as their First XV was playing in two counties in the north of England, their second team inevitably came to grief.

What they said . . .

François Pienaar: 'It was a true honour and one of the biggest thank yous of my life. When he gave me the trophy he said, "Thank you for what you have done for South Africa." And I thought, nobody has done more for the country than the President.'

Joel Stransky: 'Our coach always says that a dropped goal is an easy way of getting points. It was the obvious move, so I just said to Joost, give me the ball and I will do it.'

Kitch Christie: 'Jonah Lomu got the ball eight times and we knocked him down eight times. But even I did not realise how big he was until I saw him close up.'

Sean Fitzpatrick: 'This hurts more than losing the 1991 semi-final. The game was there for the taking. One minute before full time we had the chance to win it. We did not get the ball to Lomu enough, especially early on.'

Louis Luyt and Nelson Mandela before the final.

Sean Fitzpatrick, No. 2, and Graeme Bachop await developments at a maul.

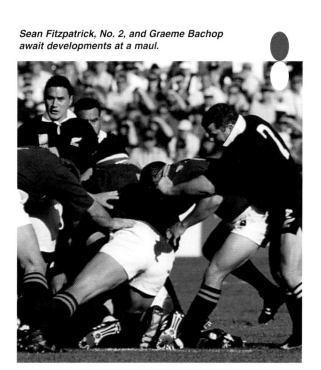

Louis Luyt (president of SARFU): 'We boasted in 1987 and 1991 that the Cup was not won because we were not there. Then in 1995 we proved that if we had been there we would have won.'

Morné du Plessis: 'There was an unbelievable force, a national surge of emotion behind the team that carried them through. We have a special talent on the field and a great defence that did not concede a try in the last two matches. But top of the list in the difference between South Africa and the other 15 teams were the dedicated, honest coach and the charismatic captain. The other teams did not have that flow of emotion.'

Laurie Mains: 'Our handling let us down. There were passing opportunities which we neglected, but even when we did pass, it was lax.'

South Africa Celebrates
What a party!
John Robbie

What a day, what a tournament and what a party! In fact the party is still going on all over the country, and probably will be until Cardiff in 1999. And why not? The World Cup finals and final were everything South Africa had dreamed of, and more. The national side did not really need to win: they had delivered the dream final to the country, the pressure was off and the victory was a bonus – but what a bonus. Driving home from Ellis Park though the hordes of celebrating people – young, old, black, white, male, female – was at times more dangerous than facing Jonah Lomu in full charge. To give a verdict on the tournament is difficult, in fact it's hard to know just where to start.

That it took place in South Africa at all is significant. Go back five years and the country was heading in the same way as Bosnia, or so it sometimes appeared. Go back to 1992 and the 'Anthem Test' against New Zealand at Ellis Park – there was little unity there, remember? The Park that day was like a political rally and the game was followed by anger, threat and counter-threat. No sign

then of President Mandela wearing a Springbok jersey and Steve Tshwete would have burned the blazer he wore so proudly in 1995. The tour that followed to France and England was a disappointment both on and off the field. The awarding of the World Cup finals to South Africa was a vote of confidence in the country, and the country repaid that confidence in full. Credit must go to the management, captain and players in the South African side. For the first time they talked to the whole nation, went out of their way to demonstrate that they were new and not old South Africans. It was so good to see. Remember the singing of both anthems and 'Shoshaloza' (an old migrant workers' song which has been adopted by other sports like soccer); remember the support for Project Masakhane (to help the development of a culture of working together) and the insistence that the side had no supporters who flew the old flag. It was refreshing, honest and it united the country.

There has been lots of talk and debate about rugby development, but what does it mean? Little black kids in

A united rainbow nation backed the South African side all the way. This unity was reflected in the crowds that flocked to see their heroes.

The razzmatazz of the closing ceremony created the perfect stage for what turned out to be, in terms of excitement, a final of gigantic proportions.

shiny new kit throwing rugby balls around while press photographers snap away merrily? No, that's good enough for some, but it's not genuine. Development has two aspects, and the World Cup has provided the first of them. It has given the country some magic. Kids now want to be Chester or Jonah or François. The SARFU has said it will give them the chance; that's the second, and they must make good their promise. The days of window-dressing to get Test matches are over and must be replaced with sincerity. Let's wait and see if the promise is kept. The success of the tournament has been a great adventure for the country itself, and indeed for the continent. How many success stories have come out of Africa recently? For tourism, for investment and for the chances of hosting other events, such as the Olympics or the soccer World Cup, the success of RWC '95 cannot be underestimated. Africa was given an event and it was staged magnificently under blue African skies. If I were a paying spectator I'd want a piece of that, especially when I heard about the exchange rate (although I'd think again if all SAA planes flew as low over Ellis Park – who pays the laundry bill for that one, I wonder?).

When all is said and done, though, the event was about rugby, and it enabled the game to reinvent itself and resell itself to the world. The semis were vital. They showed that despite bad weather the game can be gripping and also, of more importance, that an expansive, prepared, aggressive side which uses its assets well can triumph over a measured, plodding, predictable outfit which has little but superior size. That opening half-hour by the All Blacks in Cape Town was as near perfection as the game can get. In a funny way it probably cost them the World Cup as South Africa were warned and New Zealand peaked too soon. Jonah Lomu caught the imagination as no other player has done and really introduced a whole new dimension to the game. Just watch flankers and locks start to appear in back lines at all levels in all countries – 'If Jonah can do it why can't we?' It's good for the game. It is also great to see Western Samoa, Italy, Argentina and others showing that the minnows are catching up. Ireland and Wales looked light years behind. The gauntlet has been thrown down; roll on 1999.

Let's remember the tragedy of Rustenburg as well. While the triumphant leaders of the game bask deservedly in all the glory, a man called Max Brito will never play, or even walk, again. Was it bad luck or preventable? Not that it matters to Max, but it will to other players. His suffering won't have been in vain if the safety of players at all levels is re-examined and improved.

With the new TV deals the game might never be the same again. Players will certainly be professional the next time around, and quite what effect this will have on rugby, who can say? Whatever happens, the 1995 World Cup has been a highlight in the evolution of rugby and of the new South Africa. William Webb Ellis would be well pleased.

A pot of gold at the end of the rainbow
Dan Retief

It was Morné du Plessis, the Springbok team manager, who remarked after South Africa's tempestuous quarter-final victory over Western Samoa that 'miracles keep happening for the rainbow team of South Africa'. Now that the Springboks have officially secured the world champion status to which they aspired in the days before the Rugby World Cup tournament, there is ample evidence to suggest that Du Plessis was not being fanciful. That fate and fortune favoured the Springboks in their quest to win the William Webb Ellis Trophy at their first attempt is not merely conjecture. Speaking on a radio talk show two days after South Africa's victory over the All Blacks, winger James Small told the audience which had jammed the station's lines: 'I don't know what it is, but there was something guiding us. It was as though it was meant to be.'

Although winning the world championship is a tremendous achievement, the Springboks' feat will go far beyond simply establishing sporting superiority. The real benefit of staging the World Cup, and of the Springboks winning, was the tidal wave of emotion which unified a nation still tottering into a new democracy. From the colourful, cheerful and hopeful opening ceremony at Newlands, when the crowd responded enthusiastically and genuinely to the saintly qualities of President Nelson Mandela, to the moment when the country's leader appeared at the final wearing François Pienaar's No. 6 Springbok jersey, the national rugby side became a symbol of accord as South Africans, in the words of the team song 'Shosholoza', learned to 'work, work and push, push as one'.

The providential aspect to South Africa's victory is unavoidable. In April, when coach Kitch Christie named a Springbok team to take on Western Samoa, he included François Pienaar in spite of the fact that because he was recovering from knee surgery the captain had played only one other match, a hastily arranged trial, since the game against the Barbarians at Lansdowne Road early in December. In announcing his team, Christie revealed that he had decided on Hennie le Roux at fly-half ahead of Joel Stransky, because he felt that the Transvaal pivot was better suited to the type of rugby he was planning for the Springboks. But centre Brendan Venter cried off injured and, surprisingly, Christie moved Le Roux to centre and called in Stransky – the man whose name will be preserved in the annals of rugby for having kicked the dropped goal which won the World Cup for South Africa. Going into the crucial opening match against Australia at Newlands, Christie again put Le Roux at centre and Stransky at fly-half. The die had been cast.

South Africa's passage to the final was at the same time fraught with controversy and attended by good fortune. In Port Elizabeth the Springboks and Canada had to return to the dressing room for 45 minutes when the floodlights failed. A truculent mood set in when the game restarted and, although South Africa used their scrum to slowly grind out a vital 20–0 victory, the match erupted into an ugly brawl in the 70th minute which resulted in Irish referee David McHugh sending off Springbok hooker James Dalton as well as Canadian captain Gareth Rees and prop Rod Snow. Later winger Pieter Hendriks and Canada full-back Scott Stewart were also cited and suspended, but an ill-considered loophole in the tournament rules allowed South Africa to recall their talisman wing, Chester Williams, as well as a pretty competent replacement hooker in Naka Drotské. This meant that the Springboks not only had back their original first-choice left wing, but in hooker Chris Rossouw they had a substitute whose throwing in was clearly better than that of Dalton. Although Dalton's sending-off was an albatross which would haunt South Africa in both their semi-final against France and the final because of the provisions to find a winner in the event of a draw, in the end they were lucky not to have been more severely punished.

After their quarter-final against Western Samoa, in which Williams returned to score a record four tries, the Springboks had to endure oblique insinuations of racism while also counting the cost of a 42–14 victory which left full-back André Joubert with a broken bone in his hand, Joost van der Westhuizen with a damaged cartilage in his neck and Mark Andrews with severely bruised ribs – the legacy of some dangerous tackling on the part of the islanders which resulted in their full-back, Mike Umaga, being cited and suspended. Joubert, a vital element in the game plan, underwent treatment which involved spending hours submerged in a decompression chamber and the Springboks announced that he would play in the Durban semi-final against France with his left hand in a soft, protective brace.

As it turned out, the full-back's 'water training' proved appropriate: Durban was engulfed in an unseasonal deluge which forced referee Derek Bevan to declare the field dangerous for play. Yet again, the Springboks, who had taken a calculated gamble by picking lock Mark Andrews to play at No. 8 were forced to wait nervously in the dressing room. After a delay of 90 minutes the game got underway, and although South Africa made the best start to splash into the lead, it was an enormous stroke of good fortune that put them into the final – Abdel Benazzi was brought down just short of their line as the Tricolours mounted one of their famous victory surges.

In the Ellis Park climax, in which Andrews had the distinction of playing only his second game of senior rugby at No. 8 – and the first was the semi-final – fortune again smiled down on the 'Boks. Sixty thousand hearts stopped beating in the 77th minute as All Black Andrew Mehrtens received the ball in a protected pocket of space. The slick little fly-half steadied himself for what surely would have been the winning dropped goal had not the ball slewed off to the right. So South Africa survived to push the match into extra time. The Springboks feared a draw, which would have brought their disciplinary record into play. Instead they fell behind to a Mehrtens penalty in the opening seconds of extra time before Stransky held his nerve to kick what seemed a straightforward penalty from 35 metres and just off the left upright. And it was the fly-half, scorned for the 1994 tour to New Zealand, who triggered an eruption of joyous applause and the biggest street party South Africa has ever seen when his drop in the 92nd minute flew true to put the Springboks into a winning 15–12 lead.

In the end, the definitive quality of the Springboks was their muscular and unremitting tackling as well as the fact that players such as Joubert, Stransky, Van der Westhuizen, Kruger, Pienaar and Andrews had, in the epic journey of 28 post-isolation Tests, matured into players of genuine international class.

And, yes, miracles do come true. There was a pot of gold waiting at the end of the rainbow.

Back row: (left to right) Garry Pagel, Gavin Johnson, Rudolf Straeuli, Kobus Wiese, Naka Drotské, Johan Roux, Brendan Venter. Middle row: (left to right) Chester Williams, Chris Rossouw, Ruben Kruger, Johannes Strydom, Mark Andrews, Pieter du Randt, Joost van der Westhuizen, Japie Mulder. Front row: (left to right) Stephanus Swart, James Small, Kitch Christie, François Pienaar, Morné du Plessis, Joel Stransky, Gysie Pienaar, Hennie le Roux, André Joubert.

Total commitment

NEXT

Retrospective
One team, one nation
Stephen Jones

The scale of the operation could best be summed up by a part of the closing ceremony at Ellis Park, when out of the blue yonder over the stadium, sudden as lightning and, to those of us shocked below, twice as dangerous, came a Jumbo Jet. It roared overhead so low that it almost literally seemed to snap the flagpoles on top of the stands. It banked sharply and disappeared over the city. Then it made a return pass over the stadium. I did not mind being close enough to read the 'Good Luck Bokke' message painted on the bottom of the aircraft. I did not want to be close enough to read the safety-instruction card.

South Africa is a country of big gestures. In general, it staged the third Rugby World Cup well, if not brilliantly, but there were big stadia, big confrontations, big scores, big deals, big Louis Luyt and a big aircraft. It was a big time to be in the Republic. My main and most vivid impressions of the tournament are twofold. First, that South Africa, the winners, were by no means a great side. Second, it had a political and sociological significance of which not even the most optimistic proponent of the one-nation philosophy would have dreamed. I have always been suspicious of sport's alleged power to grasp whole nations. I feel that, rather lazily, we assume, for example, that the whole of New Zealand are keen and breathless followers of the All Blacks, while statistically, it is probably true that two-thirds of the population care less than a flying fish if the All Blacks win the World Cup or get wiped out in every pool match.

And I would have to admit that there would have been millions of people, especially in the predominantly black areas, for whom the World Cup simply sailed in stately fashion clean over their heads. However, it is no exaggeration to say that the tournament did bind the nation like nothing else, and that, incredibly, the sport that was until so recently the Great Satan of the country, possibly second only to the army in the black books of the non-white population, is now at the sharpest end of the process. There is no doubt that South Africa's 'one team, one nation' boast came through strongly and by the end it was ringing loudly and gloriously true. The mass-circulation newspaper

the *Sowetan* suggested as much after initial doubts.

There were some superb gestures. The maturity and the sheer good sense of the Springbok manager, Morné du Plessis, and a new and yet highly significant figure on the South African rugby scene, SARFU chief executive Edward Griffiths, were the moving forces behind the efforts of the home camp to set their sights not merely on the Webb Ellis Trophy, but on playing a part in reconciliation. The gestures and interplay between the President and the Springbok captain were breathtaking. The opening ceremony, of course, was a wondrous triumph of simplicity and potent symbolism. But it was Mandela's radiance which elevated it. One smile, one face-sizzling beam, and suddenly the World Cup was on lift-off. For the President to take the field for the presentations before the final wearing a No. 6 shirt of Pienaar's was a gesture that must have reverberated around the country, and one which clearly moved the captain himself almost beyond words. And Pienaar's post-match reaction simply and gloriously confirmed the impression that as well as being a very fine flanker, the square-shouldered South African captain is precisely the breed of emancipated, aware and statesmanlike player that the Springbok brotherhood so desperately needs. To see the South African team lined up, hands on hearts, singing 'Nkosi Sikelel 'iAfrika' before each match, bravely battling on in a language not their own, was warm enough for those of us needing signs. When you consider that it is less than three years since the 'Die Stem' incident, when the Springboks bellowed out the old anthem in contravention of an agreement and of morality, then you have to be staggered by the speed of change.

Of course, the notes of caution are justified. Some of the gloating, led by Louis Luyt, recalled the old days of South African arrogance. And while the process of reconciliation was obvious – though people like Griffiths are fully aware that this is only a totem, a colourful start, rather than the real thing of lasting rapprochement – it is also obvious that economic factors, the poverty, and the faction fighting between the ANC and the IFP will not be cooled off simply by one man lifting a trophy and one

Louis Luyt, the president of the SARFU, and Nelson Mandela greet the players before the final. The comments made by Luyt at the post-match dinner sparked a great deal of controversy.

President going, beamingly, off his trolley.

In general, though not exclusively, it was a happy World Cup. It simply consumed South Africa, the media, the senses. It was inescapable, manifested in every airport, restaurant, hotel, street, billboard, stadium, newspaper. It showed how dramatic the effects can be if you really centralise the thing, hold it in one country instead of dispersing it to the four winds with the consequent dramatic loss of impact. That is why, however successful it may be in other ways, Wales 1999 will not compare with South Africa 1995. Wales '99 should read Most Bits of Europe '99. When will they ever learn? There was unpleasantness, even if you give Luyt the benefit of the doubt and accept that he was simply, as Morné du Plessis explained, 'tired and emotional when he spoke'. There was the unpleasantness at Port Elizabeth in the match between South Africa and Canada, in which Rod Snow, the splendid Canadian prop, was preposterously ill treated in being dismissed. At least the tournament officials later threw Pieter Hendriks out of the event, because it was he who poured petrol on the burning building. There was unpleasantness because some areas of the country, even apart from the evil Johannesburg, are unsafe, and to blame foreign newspaper talk is dangerous.

I have to be perfectly frank as far as the rugby was concerned and say that it was not a vintage World Cup. It was tense, reasonably fast and exciting, but in a meaty, straight-up-and-down sort of way. The tackling was thunderous; the defensive organisation of all but the very worst teams was awesome. The kicking was out of the top drawer. Players like Thierry Lacroix, Andrew Mehrtens and Rob Andrew struck the ball beautifully, and indeed, one of the reasons why some of the games played at altitude were poor spectacles was simply that the kickers could blast the ball 80 and 90 yards in the thin air. Why on earth take the risk of trying to play the ball downfield through lots of phases when one good clinical hoof had the same effect? But there was a lack of colourful, individual brilliance. Of course, there was individual brilliance of a sort. Jonah Lomu hit the tournament like a thunderclap and after that he made ever louder impressions. To be fair, he was not just the most blockbusting runner the game has ever seen. As he showed against England in the semi-final, he has pace, a change of pace, an in-and-out swerve and he can defend on the turn, too. Mehrtens was a wonderful cool young general. On reflection, it seems to me that Cabannes and Abdel Benazzi of France just shaded Josh Kronfeld as the forward of the tournament, but it was good to see the art of openside flank play reintroduced in so emphatic a manner.

There were flashes of skill from the likes of André Joubert and Joost van der Westhuizen of the Springboks;

from Walter Little, in the middle of an incredible revival, having appeared washed-up grey rather than All Black some time ago. There was art of a different sort from the splendid Argentinian front row and their clever lock German Llanes – indeed, the Argentinian forwards must still be wondering how on this earth they did not win all three of their pool games, so clear was their superiority in the tight play. There was the excellence of John Eales, the footballing ability of Zinzan Brooke, the surprising doggedness of the Italians and, although their team was slightly over the hill, the boundless morale of the Western Samoans.

But so rarely did the event reach magical heights. It was all sweated but so rarely breathtaking. I had no doubt whatsoever that the culprits, apart from the increased fitness and endurance of the players, which shrinks the pitch, were the disastrous ruck/maul laws which, though partly repealed, still exert malign influence, still deliver the game to the defence, still clog up the field. People said that the great dazzling talents of the game, like Guscott, Lynagh, Campese, Horan, Catt, Wilson, Marcello Cuttitta, and the rare rest, must all have declined. It seems to me far too much of a coincidence that they should all have declined in the same snapshot of history. I think that rugby itself has declined, that it has declined because of some misguided notion of entertaining rugby, that continuity by itself means nothing. If rugby wants to help individual talents to thrive, and to give us those moments which remain seared in the memory, then they have to restore the game to the team going forward, award the scrum to the team making ground, and thereby recall hundreds of straying forwards to the forward battle where they belong.

Of course, there were heady, glorious moments when the final ended, when President Mandela did his stuff, when Pienaar spoke so well. Everywhere from the far north of Natal to the Cape, from Soweto to East London, wild partying broke out, and all night the noise of a country going berserk could be heard. But it was it was essentially a sad moment when Kitch Christie, the South Africa coach, was asked the key to his team's World Cup triumph. 'Defence,' he said. Of course, he was dead right. But in all our spirits, surely we require more of the World Cup-winners, this year, any year, than that they should be brilliant at nothing more elevated than defending, stopping the other lot from playing.

There is no question that South Africa deserved the win on that wonderful day at Ellis Park. But there is no doubt that they never reached in the tournament as a whole the heights of the previous winners, the 1991 Wallabies, or of the best team in South Africa in 1995 – New Zealand. The All Blacks did graft on a little adventure, did use their backs as a means of advance rather than as a simple adjunct. But there was so much to stir the blood to either joy or anger. France, inspired by Thierry Lacroix in the centre and by the gliding Emile Ntamack on the wing, came strongly, and with just 5 per cent more conviction and 10 per cent more class at half-back they could have been the champions. Certainly, because of the extra gear they had in ambition and execution it was important they they should have beaten the plodding, hidebound English in the third-place play-off. If only coach Pierre Berbizier can keep the team together; can ward off the evil, feuding spirits which traditionally buzz the French camp, he must have a fine team in the making.

The home nations failed to trouble the scorers. Ireland, Wales and Scotland were roughly on the same low level and anyone making too much of the Scottish comeback against New Zealand should, like the English celebrating their own late tries against the All Blacks, recall with a shudder their lack of competitiveness when the match was live. But at least every team in the tournament, even down to the Ivorians, had their moments. They may have been heavily defeated but they scored their tries; just as Japan, humiliated though they might have been against New Zealand, bar one dodgy penalty try decision could easily have beaten Ireland, whom they outclassed.

There was enough for everyone, I suppose. There will be joyous memories after the exhaustion has eased, especially if we could all be sanguine that the game's authorities can keep a handle on the massive boom. Would that they could trade in the lot, all the billions they have taken from the Rugby World Cup and Mr Murdoch and sponsors and spectators, just to buy one machine. The machine, technologically advanced way beyond its years, would with one burst repair spinal columns. It would restore and regenerate the spines and the movement of all the people paralysed in the sport. It would cause Max Brito, the splendid Ivorian wing who played with true defiance under pressure, to rise and walk again, to be able to touch his children, work to support his family. Let us hope that support for Max Brito lives as long as the happier memories of South Africa. Let us hope that one day, the magical machine will arrive.

MIDLAND

"Coming from the Mill" 1930 L. S. Lowry. Courtesy City of Salford Art Gallery.

How the grass roots are nourished by Midland branches

The communities around our branches are nourished by the care and concern of our staff and by substantial funds from our pre-tax profits. We pay particular attention to the inner cities, to disabled people and those socially-deprived, as well as to a host of education, training and youth projects. Despite what some people think, banking isn't always ruled by figures in the balance sheet. Just now and again, figures in the landscape get welcome priority.

The Listening Bank

Member HSBC ◆▶ *Group*

Highlights

Jonah Lomu - a human tornado
Barry John

The size, speed and power of the 20-year-old All Black proved more than just a handful for all of New Zealand's opponents.

Jonah Lomu of New Zealand was my original man of the tournament and, despite his below-par performance in the final, in which Joel Stransky's late, late dropped goal gave South Africa an historic and deserved World Cup triumph at Ellis Park, I still believe Lomu was the individual

of a magnificent competition. The world is Lomu's oyster. I cannot remember any young player — Lomu, don't forget, is the youngest All Black in history — having such a profound and immediate impact on the world stage. True, word had filtered through that the All Blacks had unearthed a real diamond, better even than Va'aiga Tuigamala at his age, but top billing like that tests the nerve and resolve of even the most experienced. Lots of players have fallen by the wayside, unable to cope with modern pressures and demands. To exceed all advance notices, as Lomu did at just 20 years of age, is unbelievable, and I have no hesitation in saying that he is one of the greatest natural talents I have ever seen.

Gareth Edwards, J.P.R. Williams and Gerald Davies were all superb athletes as well as rugby players; so too were Mike Gibson, Jo Maso and David Duckham. However, Lomu possesses an amazing range of talents and therefore offers an amazing range of alternatives. When he takes the field, his sheer presence seems to block out the sun.

His greatest World Cup moment — the best of his seven tries — was his first against England in the semi-final at Newlands. Lomu had to turn and retrieve a bad pass, a feature of the New Zealand game which was to cost them dearly in the final, some 40 yards out with three players to beat. He collected the ball and took on the English defence as though they were skittles set up for him in exactly the correct order. The last skittle, a shell-shocked Mike Catt, was exposed to an eyeball-to-eyeball confrontation with the human tornado. It was no contest. Even though Lomu stumbled, he quickly recovered, and though of Tongan rather than Maori descent he introduced poor Catt to the Maori side-step (a direct line), which left the England full-back in a bemused heap as well as registering on rugby's Richter scale.

American football and a new-look Rugby League were already offering Lomu vast fortunes — and they rarely back losers. They realised his huge box-office appeal and merchandising power. Given his tender years, he is the man for the next century and the 1995 World Cup introduced him globally: the heart-stopping final was viewed in more than 100 countries.

Which brings us to that final and Lomu's poor showing. He dropped passes, lost the ball in the tackle and was unable to provide the spark to ignite the All Blacks. For this, praise must go first to the South African coach, Kitch Christie. By conceding beforehand that Lomu needed special attention, he was effectively saying that the player was a phenomenon; that if you stopped Lomu you would reduce the All Black machine by half. Christie analysed every aspect of Lomu's game and how he was used in certain areas of the field. The defensive strategy was very practicable, and in James Small he had a gutsy character who thrives on a challenge, particularly a physical one. The fact that Small was offside most of the time and blocking off the supply line to Lomu was a practised tactic. No one complained, because it is accepted that if you can get away with anything it is a case of 'carry on'.

In addition, it was an indictment of the lack of thought and reaction by Walter Little and Frank Bunce that they did not pick up on the situation. Surely someone like Lomu can be as effective without the ball, as a decoy. He still commands the attention of at least two defenders in uncharacteristic positions, leaving space for others. The penny did eventually drop, and

Not only did François Pienaar have a magnificent tournament, he also led his side to victory and made the dream of a nation come true.

when Lomu did come on a midfield charge he was bypassed, allowing full-back Glen Osborne to make a sweeping touchline run, which was brilliantly stopped in the left-hand corner. Players of Lomu's presence and ability can be used in more than the obvious way, and that is what disappointed me about the lack of adaptability of the All Blacks' approach in the final. To maximise his remarkable talent, Lomu needs at least one thinking player around him to ensure that his involvement is varied and unpredictable.

Selecting Lomu as my player of the tournament was no easy task, and I realise there will be some flak in the air, especially after so many South Africans did so many things beyond the call of duty. The fact that André Joubert played the semi-final against France and then the final itself with a broken hand typified the South African spirit, as did their wonderful scrum-half, Joost van der Westhuizen, who went off in the semi-final with a rib injury. Whatever the damage, there was no way either was going to miss the biggest sporting event in South African history. The Springbok captain, François Pienaar, is now part of folklore, and rightly so. The way he conducted himself both on and off the field was an example to everyone. The pressure on him to succeed had been building for well over a year and many men would have cracked under that expectancy. Yet not once did he allow the ship to deviate from its intended course, and he and his team deserved their ultimate reward.

The New Zealand lock Ian Jones was another outstanding performer. Jones has been on the world circuit for six or seven years now, and that is a long time in the tough and rugged second row. His astonishing line-out display in the final was probably the best I have seen and it had the vital effect of keeping the All Blacks in the game at crucial times when they would otherwise have been struggling. France offered the exciting Emile Ntamack on the wing and a fabulous pair of flankers in Abdelatif Benazzi and Laurent Cabannes. Scotland had their incomparable captain, Gavin Hastings, playing in his last internationals.

Yet I can do no other than stick with Jonah Lomu. Time will tell whether my decision is justified, but there is no doubt in my mind that Lomu, given the correct support players and used properly, can lift a game into another stratosphere. And I will be able to say 'I was there' when a truly remarkable career unfolds in the years to come.

New Zealand beaten, but still the best
Bill Beaumont

So South Africa won the World Cup, and deservedly so, but I have to stick with New Zealand as my team of the tournament because they were the best rugby-playing side there and gave the rest an exhilarating lesson in how the game could be approached with an emphasis on ambition and flair. The Springboks battled superbly, and I admired the way they stopped the All Blacks in the final and the tenacity and will to win that characterised their play all the way through the tournament. But they did not really win it on pure rugby ability. In the final New Zealand played a naive game and paid the price.

Unfortunately, some of the younger All Blacks allowed the pressure to get to them, and in the end Andrew Mehrtens, who could have tied it up for them with his drop-kicking, could not find the target when it mattered. They just seemed to hope to feed the ball to Jonah Lomu and expected him to do the rest without working out anything much by way of an alternative. And on the day, the big wing froze.

While the Blacks were bottling it, the 'Boks showed the way to play when you have your backs to the wall. It had happened in the semi-final against France at King's Park, and it happened again in the final at Ellis Park. The fact that they could finish as they did in both games was a tremendous credit to them. We can now see that, odd as it may seem, the kind of game the All Blacks were trying to play suited South Africa. They set out their defensive stall very well and closed New Zealand down – something no other side managed to do in any of their previous five World Cup matches.

But even accepting the Springboks' many attributes, I must go with the All Blacks for bringing a refreshing style to the World Cup that showed there is nothing preordained about percentage rugby. If anything, percentage rugby for the All Blacks – in the sense of the rugby best suited to winning them matches – was what we witnessed in South Africa. Glen Osborne at full-back was an exceptional runner with the ball, if a little naive at

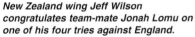

New Zealand wing Jeff Wilson congratulates team-mate Jonah Lomu on one of his four tries against England.

Full-back Glen Osborne proved to be an exciting runner throughout the World Cup.

times. Jonah Lomu, Jeff Wilson and, let's not forget him, Marc Ellis, were as high-quality wings as you could hope to see. Lomu received all the publicity, but Wilson is a superb all-round footballer and a precious asset to any squad. In midfield, Frank Bunce and Walter Little were such strong-running attackers and such hard-tackling defenders that they could equally well have played in the back row. Look what happened when they met England: Jeremy Guscott misses one tackle and off they go and score.

It is great to see New Zealand, whom I have always regarded as dour, uncompromising and workmanlike, efficiency being the whole tenor of their game, throwing up an outside-half with the exciting qualities of the 22-year-old Andrew Mehrtens, who seems more in the Australian or French mould. He was truly outstanding, although for the rest of his life he will remember the dropped goal he missed two minutes from time. The great surprise to me was that one so young could choose so many right options so often. He would surely wish to give credit to the quick hands of Graeme Bachop inside him, although I would be critical of Bachop for kicking too much during the last 20 minutes of normal time in the final. He played into South Africa's hands by going for line-outs – remember that the Springboks won three defensive balls in a row towards the end. I felt he would have been better keeping the ball in hand.

What New Zealand should have done was adapted from the England game and not simply thought that all they had to do was to approach the final exactly as they had the semi-final. A look at South Africa's defensive pattern throughout the World Cup showed how tightly they could close a game down, but the New Zealanders seemed to imagine that they could beat everyone else as they had beaten England. When they came to Ellis Park they scarcely tried a back-row move all afternoon.

This is not a reflection of their talent. In the semi-final they had highlighted every one of the English weaknesses in the first five minutes. Craig Dowd certainly destroyed the England scrum, and indeed, he was a fine prop throughout the World Cup. Olo Brown was steady on the other side of the scrum, and Sean Fitzpatrick threw in exceptionally well. Ian Jones is a great athlete, a sensational line-out leaper who won consistent and vital ball against both England and South Africa. Alongside him, Robin Brooke was a good, solid grafter but the All Blacks need another big man in the line-out, another decent presence to take some of the onus off Jones.

In the back row, Josh Kronfeld on the open side was another who made a dramatic entry, even if in the final he tended to fade away after a first good half. My main concerns about this New Zealand pack focus on the blind side and No. 8, where Mike Brewer or Jamie Joseph or Zinzan Brooke do not make a consistent contribution. Brooke is particularly guilty. After producing an endlessly influential performance in the semi-final, he was almost invisible in the final. The Springboks would not let him take a hold of the game and he made the mistake of standing out of defensive scrums, thereby giving South Africa confidence and impetus, which ultimately meant they were awarded some important penalties.

If this seems critical, it is only because I was so disappointed that the All Blacks were unable to repeat their earlier form when it came to the match which mattered more than any of the others. If you take the broad picture of the entire month, they were a joy, lovely to watch, with every last player wanting to run with the ball. If you accept that their weaknesses are at 6 and 8, then imagine how good they could be by the 1999 World Cup if those problem areas can be addressed.

But full marks to South Africa for going one better than New Zealand by winning the tournament. They were supremely motivated, especially by the gentleman who presented them with the trophy at the end, but then Nelson Mandela was the man of this World Cup, wasn't he?

Along with Jonah Lomu, one of New Zealand's greatest finds was Andrew Mehrtens. For a player of so little international experience, he made the right decision time and time again.

My World XV
Fergus Slattery

15 André Joubert (South Africa)
14 Emile Ntamack (France)
13 Japie Mulder (South Africa)
12 Walter Little (New Zealand)
11 Jonah Lomu (New Zealand)
10 Andrew Mehrtens (New Zealand)
 9 Joost van der Westhuizen (South Africa)
 1 Matias Corral (Argentina)
 2 Féderico Mendez (Argentina)
 3 Patricio Noriega (Argentina)
 4 Ian Jones (New Zealand)
 5 John Eales (Australia)
 6 Laurent Cabannes (France)
 8 François Pienaar (South Africa, captain)
 7 Josh Kronfeld (New Zealand)

Imagine the very best of the 1995 World Cup and you can start to picture a fabulous dream team made up of a pack to make my old forward's heart sing and backs who, while they might not quite match the pack in my Utopian rating, are rather useful for all that.

I would have liked to have put Gavin Hastings at full-back because of the great inspiration he was to the Scotland team, but you have to accept that André Joubert was clearly the best – and clearly the most consistent – throughout the tournament. His performances in the semi-final and final, when he played with a broken hand, were staggering. I have experience of playing in the Five Nations with a broken hand in a cast but, unlike the South African, I did not disclose it. I know exactly what the implications of this injury were, but they did not seem to

The technique of the Argentinian front row, Corral, Mendez and Noriega, caused problems for every side they faced.

affect him. He was elegant, balanced, pacy and composed – an ideal combination.

Jonah Lomu on one wing was the easiest choice of all, in spite of the fact that he had a difficult final for New Zealand against South Africa. Even in the final I felt he played well – it was just that the expectations of him were so great. He had demonstrated throughout the tournament that he was a magnificent runner, aided by his great partner, Josh Kronfeld. They were like two nuns: wherever Lomu went, so did Kronfeld. Lomu's problem is that he needs to remain athletic and fit, to keep his weight down and maintain his pace, and that will involve great personal discipline.

For my other wing, Emile Ntamack is an obvious choice and I was delighted to see the emergence of players such as the Frenchman and Lomu in a tournament during which a lot of others, notably David Campese, were reaching the end of their careers. Ntamack comes fast off both feet and although his winning try against Scotland was essentially a team effort, he still had to break through two men to score.

Centre play was generally a disappointment. Lacroix and Sella hardly shone as runners, though that had a lot to do with the selections at fly-half; England did not seem geared to using Carling and Guscott. So I have gone for the best defensive centre, Japie Mulder, and the best attacker, Walter Little. Mulder's tackling, not least when facing Little in the final, was massive, but perhaps this is a choice some would not agree with. New Zealanders would doubtless want Frank Bunce alongside Little, but my final World Cup XV contains only four South Africans and they, after all, are the champions, and for me Mulder deserves his place. He complements Little, who is another fine tackler but a player who brings greater subtlety than his South African counterpart to the running and passing aspects of centre play. Little is another of my choices who stood up well to the rigours of the tournament by never allowing his level of performance to drop.

I have no qualms about making another All Black, Andrew Mehrtens, my fly-half. Mehrtens improved as the tournament went on. He is a lovely runner with a lot of pace who is eager to keep the ball in hand but also kicks well, whether tactically or for goal. He is one of the new boys on the block and fully merits selection in the dream team even though years of development still lie ahead for him.

Joost van der Westhuizen is my scrum-half, but in many ways he is lucky to get in ahead of his opponent in

John Eales competes with England's Martin Johnson. For long periods of that game the Australians dominated line-out possession.

the final, Graeme Bachop. The South African's major weakness is that, while he is a very good athlete, very fast, very brave, and has a wonderful pass, he is a ratty player. He showed it on a number of occasions during the World Cup, most notably in the fracas with the Canadians. He has to learn to keep a cool head, otherwise he will cause problems in the future. If I were an opposing flanker, it is something I would play on, enticing him into the web of indiscipline.

I am much more excited about my forward selection than I am about the backs, simply because this is a pack which is so mobile that it would be a joy for anyone to play in it. To start with, I go for an all-Argentinian front row: Matias Corral, Féderico Mendez and Patricio Noriega. In the World Cup they revealed themselves as wonderful handlers, tremendously physical players and quite exceptional scrummagers. So not only did they perform their basic function better than any other unit in the tournament, they also contributed immensely in the loose. You cannot ask for more from tight forwards than that.

My selection in the second row of Ian Jones and John Eales might be questioned because both are number 4 jumpers, but they were comfortably the best locks in the tournament and none of the more recognised number 2 jumpers impressed me enough to make me contemplate a different choice. In any case, Jones has played quite a lot for New Zealand at 2, the Australians move Eales around to all points of the line-out, and both are superb practitioners in the shortened line-out, an important area where they would dominate quite easily.

Josh Kronfeld, to me, was the best forward of the World Cup and my other choice at flanker, Laurent Cabannes, is the only player I also picked when I carried out the same exercise at the end of the 1991 tournament. Cabannes, I felt, was a more mature and better player this time than four years earlier, bouncing back strongly from a disappointing season at home during which his fitness was suspect. Kronfeld had stamina and speed, not least when tracking Lomu, and adopted the correct role of the flanker by staying out of trouble in order to create trouble. His support play was astonishingly astute, both in attack and defence, and it was to his great credit that he did so well in defence in the final after contributing so much in attack in the previous matches.

For my No. 8 I have looked at people like Philippe Benetton, Zinzan Brooke and even Dean Richards, but I came to the conclusion that none of them was truly

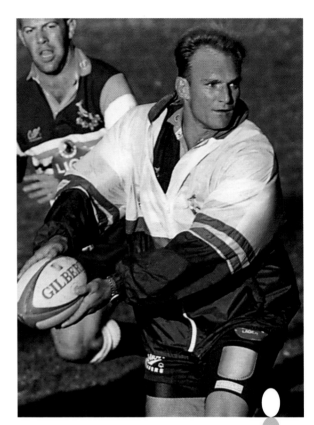

François Pienaar, the choice as captain.
He was an inspiration to both team and country
throughout South Africa's World Cup campaign.

outstanding. Brooke is perhaps the most obvious, catching the eye with his dropped goal in New Zealand's semi-final against England, but he had a poor final. Besides, I could not leave out François Pienaar. He had such an enormous impact on the tournament and his inspirational qualities as a leader were so important that I am including him in my team in the unlikely position of No. 8 and also as my captain. Pienaar is an icon. Right from the outset of the World Cup he showed himself to be an extremely good ambassador, almost going beyond the bounds of the purpose for which he was put there. In the special atmosphere of South Africa in 1995 he was called upon to do much more than most captains have ever been asked to do or would ever have done.

Pienaar is not a flash player, but he is there at the coalface, very committed and hard-working and totally honest. For me that quality is what makes him such an excellent captain. I can afford to have both him and Kronfeld in my back row because I have Eales and Jones at the line-out. There you have it: every eventuality taken care of in my 1995 dream team.

Controversial moments of Rugby World Cup '95
Andy Irvine

The 1995 World Cup was the best there has been but a tournament of this magnitude is bound to have its controversial moments and I suppose for most people the brawl between South Africa and Canada in Port Elizabeth will stand out above any of the others. It is a disgrace that a game can degenerate this way and I would have to say that the initially guilty parties were the Canadians. Their full-back, Scott Stewart, was completely out of order and in the end I felt sorry for the Springbok hooker, James Dalton, when he was sent off. Although he was worked up in the heat of the moment, I am sure he was only trying to look after his team-mates and it was one of the saddest moments of the tournament to see him with his head in his hands, knowing that his World Cup was over. It was doubly bitter for him when South Africa won the final.

A lot of people said it served Dalton right, but when I was playing we knew who the dirty players were and we

The end of the World Cup for South Africa's James Dalton and Canada's Gareth Rees when they are dismissed for their part in the brawl which dampened the Pool A decider.

knew, too, that there were sneaky ones who were never spotted. I have more sympathy for those who boil over on the spur of the moment than for those who act premeditatedly. Nevertheless, I give considerable credit to Rugby World Cup for the way they responded to the incident and for having the nerve to act retrospectively after viewing the video evidence – not only in suspending

the sent-off players, Dalton, Gareth Rees and Rod Snow, but also in citing Pieter Hendriks and, of course, Stewart, and banning them as well. In doing so, the organisers set a standard of discipline for others at the World Cup.

The use of video evidence is a significant step forward. In fact, I would offer the referees, too, the benefit of video analysis in certain situations, for instance,

Chester Williams scored four tries on his return to the South African side, made possible only by the suspension of Pieter Hendriks.

The Tongans before their match against France, in which Feleti Mahoni (No.6) was sent off, although it was his captain, Manakaetau 'Otai (No.8), who was the guilty party. Mahoni was sent straight home after the game.

forward pile-ups. The tries – or non-tries – by Abdel Benazzi for France against South Africa and Ruben Kruger for South Africa against New Zealand were other controversial moments which could have been resolved to everyone's satisfaction by this means. In spite of the growing significance of the results of rugby matches, I would say that once or twice in ten games, even big games, the wrong side win because of refereeing errors. Suppose Andrew Mehrtens had kicked a couple more goals in the final and New Zealand had sneaked it by three points. There would have been all hell let loose about Kruger's try. I have a great deal of sympathy for referees for having to make split-second decisions and I just wonder whether the American football policy, whereby they take a look at the video before final decisions are made, could be adopted in rugby. It all depends on how seriously you want to take the game, of course.

There was a further postscript the the South African bans. If you were cynical, you could say that the Springboks were quite happy that Hendriks was out of the tournament because it allowed them to bring back their best wing, Chester Williams, who was absent from the original squad through injury.

While the events of the South Africa–Canada match were a major issue, I personally felt that the most controversial incident of the lot was the sending-off in the

Tonga–France game. First, the player who was dismissed, Feleti Mahoni, was the wrong one: the man who should have gone was the Tongan captain, Mana 'Otai. Second, although Tonga had the opportunity to pursue the matter, it dawned on them that someone would have to be punished and it was better that that someone was Mahoni rather than the captain.

The South Africans ran a wonderful World Cup, but the celebrations were soured at the end by Louis Luyt's speech at the closing dinner. We will never really know whether his suggestion that South Africa would have won the two previous tournaments had they taken part was simply made in jest, as he claimed, or whether he was being a drunk, boorish Afrikaner. But the New Zealand walk-out led by Colin Meads and Brian Lochore summed up the reaction to his remarks. I was told that, after Mike Brewer had spoken to him, Luyt was asked whether it was a conversation or a confrontation and replied, 'It depends how you interpret "Big Afrikaner bastard".' Quite honestly, I do not think South Africa would have had a sniff in the first World Cup, in which there was no one to match the New Zealanders. The 1991 World Cup is more difficult to assess because New Zealand had lost it a bit. Nevertheless, Australia were in great form. And it is quite a different proposition to play in a World Cup on your home territory, as the All Blacks found to their cost least six or seven times out of ten to the All Blacks – and they would win with a great deal more style.

The most terrible tragedy of the World Cup was the appalling injury to Ivorian Max Brito. Yet I would not agree with the view that it was in some way caused by a mismatch between the Ivory Coast and Tonga. On the issue of whether the minnows should be permitted to take on the big fish, I believe that, on balance, less experienced teams should have the opportunity to play against the world leaders – even if they are going to get a whipping. I felt it was a dreadful coincidence that the Max Brito injury occurred when a particularly physical side were playing one of the small fry. The Ivory Coast do not necessarily lack skill, just size, and even then their forwards were quite big.

What I would like to see is a lot more common sense in team selection. In my view it was totally wrong for Scotland to put out their top Test side against Ivory Coast. I thought that was a disgrace – and it is also a disgrace for a country to take a squad of 26 to a World Cup and then not give them all a game. Three of the Scottish lads did not play at all. I wonder whether the organisers should consider making it compulsory for teams to give everyone at least one game. To me it is completely outside the spirit of rugby to expect someone to train at home and then go on pre-tournament training camps only to do nothing more than sit on the bench.

The tragedy of the World Cup. Referee Don Reordan summons a stretcher for the injured Max Brito. It was a moment that marred everyone's enjoyment of the rugby spectacle that was taking place.

in South Africa. Moreover, I am not convinced that South Africa were the best team in this tournament. True, they won the final, and on the day they were at least equal to the New Zealanders. But it is heartbreaking that games should be decided on penalty kicks and dropped goals and I am sure that Springbok–All Black games would go at

Scotland's 89-0 thrashing of the Ivory Coast was a record score in the World Cup until it was beaten by New Zealand nine days later. Should Scotland have played their inexperienced squad members instead?

Interviews
The man in the No.6 shirt
Morné du Plessis

After about 20 minutes of watching New Zealand play England, I thought that there was no way that we would beat the All Blacks. Well, we've got this far, I reasoned, we might as well enjoy it, but that was the limit of my ambitions at that moment in time. On the Monday morning Kitch Christie just started nibbling away at the guys and away we went on another week of wonderful discoveries.

There were several reasons why we managed to win the World Cup. One of the primary ones was the faith, and deep, deep faith it was, of Kitch. From the very first day he took over the reins he believed that the side had the potential to win the tournament. Eventually that sort of conviction gets embedded in a person. So it wasn't just when we got to the semi-final that we began to think we were in with a chance – the team always thought that

Coach Kitch Christie, Webb Ellis Trophy in hand, shares his delight with the South African players.

because they believed in Kitch and he believed in them.

My own perspective was different. I had been in the rugby wilderness for so many years. Then, six months earlier, I got a call one Monday afternoon and was given five minutes to make up my mind about whether I wanted to come on board. I didn't know what to think, but somewhere deep inside I sensed that here was an opportunity, just a small one, to make some difference to something. It was no more definite or tangible than that. I felt the job would not just be one of sitting in endless committee meetings, but would entail something altogether more substantial. I guess I was right, although I'm still trying to make sense of it all.

The scale of what we did manage to achieve in the country and for the country was way beyond my wildest dreams. The magnitude of it all was nothing to do with me – it came about because the team and the country wanted it. Before the guys went on to the field for the final I told them that very few people in a lifetime get a chance to make a difference to something in history beyond their little sports field. They had created that opportunity, even if it were only small and fleeting. They had to go out there and take it. That is why we tried to remain humble in victory. We knew that glory would be transient and could so easily have passed us by. We knew how fragile any team's claims on glory are. We weren't in the World Cup in either 1987 to 1991, and even if we had been I doubt very much whether we would have achieved anything then.

What this team had to offer was nothing out of the ordinary in that its attributes – power, fitness, endurance, commitment, self-belief and a little bit of luck – were time-honoured ones. Maybe what set us apart was the emotion with which we played. As François Pienaar said immediately after the final, 'There were not 62,000 cheering us on out there. There were 43 million.' It's true that from somewhere a wonderful bond built up between the team and the nation. It was no gimmick, not a stage-managed thing, it just happened. A lot of the credit for that must go to François. He is a very special captain and a very special man. The players needed him very badly on many occasions. I think his sincere worth and status was shown in the way that he was embraced as a figurehead by President Mandela. There really was something special between them.

It was such a great moment for the team when the President came into the changing room just 45 minutes before the kick-off. Mr Mandela could not believe how calm we were. He was wearing François's No. 6 jersey and the look which passed between them conveyed a depth of feeling which just could not have been contrived. What an advantage the President's presence gave us over the All Blacks. In fact, this whole squad was very genuine and very ordinary, and I mean that in a positive, complimentary, sense. There were no special team talks, no magic tricks, just good old-fashioned belief in each other and what lay before them. It was this quality which helped sustain them through the low points. And believe me, there were low points throughout the whole tournament. We did not have one trouble-free match. The opening game against Australia was something else entirely. From that great high we hit rock-bottom against Romania. The final pool match, against Canada, was a disaster. I was on my way down to the pitch when it all started. I knew something bad had happened because two Canadian supporters hurled abuse at me. I couldn't understand how they could get so worked up. Again we had to regroup and find our way back.

The quarter-final against Western Samoa was the most physical of all the matches. Of course, the final itself was intense, but in terms of sheer physical contact, it was the quarter-final which did the damage. On to the semi-final and the rains of Durban. All that anxiety and then just holding out at the end – believe me, I'm not sure I could live through another six weeks like it.

It may be hard for people on the outside to appreciate the peaks and troughs a squad goes through. It may look all plain sailing to them, but let me tell you that just two days before the final we were at crisis point. We were making a short hotel transfer across Johannesburg and the guys were all on their cellphones taking calls from people wanting tickets and it was bedlam. Kitch called a halt to it all. The week up to that point had been too big and too long for us. Perhaps we needed this little crisis, with people all over the place, shouting and getting distracted. From that moment on, a silence fell and the quiet mood, the one President Mandela remarked upon, returned. Again, full credit for that goes to Kitch Christie.

For some reason at the final I felt the calmest I had felt in the entire six weeks. I knew then that the inevitable would happen. If it had been us who lost by a dropped goal in extra time, then I sincerely feel that the squad would not have reacted too differently from the way they did in victory. They have would been disappointed, for sure, but not devastated. I think the World Cup taught them a lot about sport and about themselves.

Morné du Plessis, the South African team manager.

That special feeling of ultimate triumph
André Joubert

It would be impossible to exaggerate the combination of pride and joy – sheer ecstatic joy – that the World Cup represented for all of us in the South African team. It was a feeling enhanced by the knowledge that our achievements were made on behalf of all the people of our country and that we have even helped its development. What it means to me personally pales into insignificance in comparison, but even so it was a specific landmark for me, because in all my ten years of playing first-class rugby I had never been a cup-winner. Natal's Currie Cup success was achieved while I was still playing for the Free State, and I had never known that special feeling of ultimate triumph.

So I felt on top of the world for the first time in my rugby-playing life. For all of us in the Springbok team, the full realisation of what we had done came only with the passage of time. I suppose I now have an idea what people like Boris Becker and André Agassi felt when they won Wimbledon or what it was like for our own Ernie Els when he won the US Open. It is an almost indescribable sensation.

The feeling of bringing South Africa together, of the wider responsibility in our hands, made the weeks of the tournament an intensely moving experience for those of us privileged to have been a part of it. When we were driving around in our bus and saw everyone at the side of the road waving at us and cheering us on, it brought home to us forcibly that we were back in the world. When we saw Nelson Mandela entering Ellis Park wearing the No. 6 jersey of François Pienaar, everyone had a lump in his throat. The moment when we were standing on the pitch as the President walked on and the crowd started chanting his name was quite extraordinary. I hope – I am sure – that our victory will help to accelerate the development programme for rugby throughout our country. All the top players were already involved and our commitment must remain if we are to tap fully the vast resources out there. There are great footballers in South Africa, with impressive skills and powerful physiques, and if we can interest black people in our game I have no doubt many will become great rugby players as well.

It was a hard road for the Springboks to get this far. We have been back on the international scene for the last three years and we were a bit behind when we started off. We took hidings against Australia and England, and even now that we have won the Webb Ellis Trophy, there is still plenty of room for improvement. Frankly, we are just happy to be back in contact with the other countries after our years of isolation, and in that sense, the World Cup is a bonus, albeit the biggest one we could conceivably have had. I myself very nearly did not make it through the World Cup. I know how close I was to losing my battle for fitness. When I came off the field during our quarter-final against Western Samoa at Ellis Park, I immediately knew my hand was broken and when it was X-rayed things seemed even worse – it was broken in three places. It went through my mind that my World Cup had just ended, but before I had the chance to dwell on my disappointment the doctor astonished me by telling me that there was a 50 per cent chance I'd be able to play again in the tournament.

That gave me hope, but it was a bit hard to believe. I just thanked the Lord that it worked out after I spent time in a decompression chamber in Pretoria and wore a support during the matches. I was incredibly lucky, as well as incredibly anxious, before going into the semi-final against France at King's Park. I really had no idea, beyond the reassurance of the doctors, of how the broken hand would stand up to actual match play, and I could not help but ask myself if I was doing the right thing. If I had had to leave the field after five or ten minutes I would have been letting the side down. I had no power in my forefinger, which was why it was strapped to my middle finger, and no real clue as to how I would get on. As it turned out, I never felt a thing and never had any pain, either against France or in the final against New Zealand, although I did need an operation to set the bone on the day after we had won the Cup. The torrential rain in Durban also made the covering very slippery and awkward.

The final seemed a long way from our first match against Australia. Rugby is a team game, and we went out

André Joubert in action for South Africa in the opening game of the tournament against Australia.

and won that opening game as a team, which, I suppose, was the main quality that carried us through the entire tournament. To beat the Wallabies is a fine achievement in itself and it immediately put us on track because we knew that if we could beat them, not only did we have an easier route to the final, but also that we could beat anyone else as well. When it came to the final it was all on a plate for us. We were serious underdogs, and very pleased to be so. I was very happy with my form, and although I am 31, I was, and still am, enjoying my rugby as much as ever. I have battled with problems over many years – problems which kept me out for a season and a half – but for the past two seasons I have been injury-free and it has made a massive difference to my enjoyment and with it my whole rugby-playing career.

Against New Zealand, when the end of normal time came and the score stood at 9–9 with extra time lying ahead of us, it was the support of the people watching that uplifted us, that wall of sound which greeted us. During those moments before the additional 20 minutes began, I felt I could have gone on for another hour, even though it had already been such a physically demanding game. It was all about placing pressure on the All Blacks, and we did it in the last ten minutes, when it counted more than at any other time. When Joel dropped the winning goal I was standing about 4 metres to his right and was perfectly placed to experience the ecstatic moment when the ball went between the uprights. Like everyone else, I threw my hands skywards, but at the end I nearly jumped out of my skin even though, by that stage, my calves were beginning to cramp. When the whistle blew, suddenly I could not feel a thing.

Too many mistakes
Laurie Mains

We made too many mistakes in the World Cup final and that was enough to lose us the game to South Africa and leave us terribly disappointed after we had gone through the tournament so well. The South Africans defended very well but our passing was lax and we dropped the ball too many times in situations where, in other games, we had held on to it and won. Those few mistakes stopped us getting our game going because it is based fundamentally on good, precise handling. There may have been some opportunities for us to pass the ball when we did not, but more important than that, it was the hands that let us down rather than what we tried to do with the ball, especially when we dropped it when there was no pressure on us. They were not forced errors.

It was a sad ending for us. We were pretty pleased to have been underrated beforehand because it let us go about our business without too many people taking too much notice of us. Right from the beginning, when I started in 1992, we planned a four-year strategy in which our first decision was what sort of rugby New Zealand would have to play to be successful at the 1995 World Cup. We looked back on our 1987 and 1991 campaigns, decided what we wanted and then realised we could not play it that way for four years because then everyone would know what we were going to do and would work out how to counter us. So we decided to try out a few different tactics and game plans along the way. However, if you look back to our Scotland Test in 1993, which we won 51–15, you will see some similarities. There were games in which we tried things out and then did not use them again so that people would not twig. We did not intend to lose any Tests but winning a particular Test was not the ultimate goal and we were not prepared to show our hand. We did not finally refine our style until quite soon before the tournament, because if the players had known specifically what they were going to do six months earlier it would have been old hat by the time we got to South Africa.

The next thing we had to do was find players who could cope not only with the style of the game but also with Test match rugby. We quite deliberately went through a number of players over the years. We were quite ready to experiment with players rather than attempt to settle on a combination and tell ourselves that this was the team that would take us through to the World Cup.

Obviously there was a nucleus of players, but in our final year, 1994, we needed to find four players during our National Championship; full-back, wing, fly-half and openside flanker. We found them in Glen Osborne, Jonah Lomu, Andrew Mehrtens and Josh Kronfeld.

There were hours and hours of going to games and studying videotapes to see who had the skills we were looking for. Then it was a matter of making it work. I asked for four four-day training camps over our summer in which we had to build team culture and the will to succeed, finishing off with perfecting a few basic tactics and techniques that would allow our game plan to work.

We had to have quick ball and to develop the technique of delivering that quick ball without it being spoiled by opposing players wanting to slow down the game. England in the semi-final posed a huge threat because Richards, Clarke and Rodber were the biggest loose-forward combination in world rugby and also had a reputation for shutting options down. We needed to make sure they could not do that. We knew if we could deal with the England back row there would not be another back row who could make it any more difficult for us. We could have taken as big a forward pack as England's to the tournament; we have a few huge players, but they did not fit into our game plan. We were influenced by the changes in the laws, and by the realisation that New Zealand does not automatically have the biggest or strongest pack in world rugby any more. Of course, you cannot play any sort of rugby if the tight forwards do not do their job. So we never strayed from the basics of hard work and technique. Because we are smaller than most of our opposition, our techniques have to be better than theirs.

There is another important point: our rugby administrators have an acute awareness that we have to make our game a spectacle. In the UK they do not, because whatever happens the population base means they can fill Twickenham many times over. In New Zealand we have only 3 million people and Australia has a minor audience for Rugby Union, so between us we accept the need to make it an entertainment. But it goes further than that: I believe that if players are stimulated by playing the most enjoyable rugby they can play, then you are going to get more out of them.

Doing all this has not been easy and there was impatience and criticism at home. Many times I asked myself why I needed all this. A lot of the public pressure in New Zealand was brought about by ignorance of what we were doing and by factions with their own agendas. Auckland are a law unto themselves. They were interested not in who was going to do the best job at the World Cup but in getting one of their own there. There are people prepared to undermine the All Blacks to get their own way. But it was good for the All Blacks to see me having to withstand that pressure. They saw that if I had to take it, then so did they, and they came to my assistance at crucial times. It put the players and me on a level playing field because they could see that I had to go through the same rigours as they did.

We might have lost the World Cup final but there is much more to come from this team. A World Cup tournament is as good as two years' Test experience and the fact is that this team has not played together often enough to be at its absolute best. They are like the All Black side that won the 1987 World Cup: they were at their best in 1989.

Irrespective of what happened against South Africa, I would be confident that we are leaving behind the structure for another very, very strong era in New Zealand rugby.

Laurie Mains outlines his strategy during a pre-final press conference. There was little doubt that he had created the tournament's most creative side.

Proud to be part of it
Ed Morrison

What were your thoughts coming into the tournament?

Rather like the players, my sole aim was to make it past the pool matches. The number of referees was to be reduced then from 26 to 14, and the only thing on your mind was not being on the plane home the day after they made the announcement.

What are the criteria?

No one really knows. There is no discussion between the referees and the appointments panel for the simple reason that it could place too great a strain on the relationship between the two if there were constant dialogue. Marks are awarded for each referee in each game, but again none of this comes back to you at the time. It doesn't worry me too much because, like a player, you know when you've done well and when you haven't. You don't really need someone to go through every last detail with you.

Is the system fair?

It's fair in that the best referees do seem to go through to the final stages, but very unfair in that there is such a brutal cut-off point. Some of the guys from the smaller countries – and I say this with all due respect to them – would probably have known that they would be going home after the pool matches, but for the rest it comes as a shock. One minute you're in; the next you're out. The names were simply read out at the hotel on the Monday after the group games finished. It put a dampener on things. I would rather that the World Cup selected a smaller bunch of officials in the first place and then let them take care of everything. There is also a theory that if you know there is so much riding on your performance then you will referee for the assessor rather than for the match. It doesn't affect me, but I can see that the point is valid.

In which games did you officiate in the pool rounds?

I refereed New Zealand–Wales and ran the touch for France–Tonga.

Did you have any predetermined strategy?

We'd had several meetings through the year to determine broad guidelines, and then we met the team managers and coaches in Cape Town. The only specific change was that the step out of the line-out was banned. The managers weren't too happy about this amendment being made so late in the day, but in the end I didn't feel that it made too much difference. The really good thing to come out of all this is that the International Board have decided to make such meetings an annual event, involving players, coaches and referees.

What is your own philosophy of refereeing?

The whole game is potentially far too complex. My aim is to simplify it as much as possible, otherwise it can become very frustrating. Basically, you want a game to flow to enable the players to express themselves. In many ways, I find it easier to referee southern hemisphere sides, especially the All Blacks, simply because their basic skills are better than those of most sides in the northern hemisphere. They're very good in particular at recycling the ball, so that when a player goes into contact you can see it emerging fairly quickly.

When did you learn about your appointment for the final?

Not until the Monday before the game. I was just very happy to have got into the knock-out stages. I did the France–Ireland quarter-final and, again, thought I had a reasonable game. After that so much depends on who beats whom. If England had defeated New Zealand, for example, then David Bishop would probably have refereed the final and I would have taken the third-fourth play-off. It was good to have only a few days' notice because you just went out there and got on with it, and didn't have time to build up any preconceived ideas as to what might happen.

Was the final something special, or just another game?

It was a dream come true, of course. There are some

guys who think they should referee only World Cup finals all their careers, but I like to think that I'm not like that. In another sense, though, you have to see it as just another game, because if you get too worked up you're not going to referee as you normally do. My attitude was to go out there and enjoy it, because I was never going to get another opportunity like that.

How did it go?

I was fairly pleased with the way it all went. I certainly enjoyed it, although the pressure was such that the enjoyment did not come until a few days later, when it all sank in.

What makes a good game from a referee's point of view?

One in which everyone just gets on with it. Here it helped enormously that there were two very strong captains on the field in François Pienaar and Sean Fitzpatrick. They would not tolerate any ill-discipline from their men simply because they both knew it could cost them the match.

What were the critical decisions in the match?

The All Blacks scrum was under pressure early on so I had to tell Fitz that if it went down again we'd be moving under the posts for a penalty try. The other big moment occurred when the Springboks drove Kruger over the line. There was a mass of bodies and it was impossible to see whether or not the ball had been grounded. In fact it was an easy decision to make, because if you can't see it, you can't give it. If you wait too long for the bodies to unravel you don't know for sure that someone has not wriggled a hand in somehow.

And extra time?

I was just hoping that it would not come down to some silly technical offence. I was delighted that it was a dropped goal which settled it, although if you had to award a penalty, then you would award it. The Springboks seemed the more tired – Pienaar kept asking me how long there was to go even though he could see the stadium clock – yet they held on.

What was your reaction to the Louis Luyt speech?

Others were offended but it didn't bother me one bit. I felt sorry for Derek Bevan for being dragged into it all. I knew I'd done all right and that, in the end, is all you should go by. It had been a fabulous tournament and I was just proud to have been part of it.

Derek Bevan watches from the touchline as Ed Morrison has a quiet word with Joost van der Westhuizen during the World Cup final.

IT TAKES KNOWLEDGE, COMMUNICATION AND INNOVATION TO STAY AT THE TOP.

Best wishes from one great team to the others.

Statistics
World Cup Records (final stages only)
UNISYS

Highest scores:

145	New Zealand v Japan (Bloemfontein, 1995)	
89	Scotland v Ivory Coast (Rustenburg, 1995)	
74	New Zealand v Fiji (Christchurch, 1987)	

Biggest winning margins:

128	New Zealand v Japan (Bloemfontein, 1995)
89	Scotland v Ivory Coast (Rustenburg, 1995)
64	New Zealand v Italy (Auckland, 1987)

Most points by a player in a match:

45	S. Culhane (New Zealand v Japan, 1995)
44	G. Hastings (Scotland v Ivory Coast, 1995)
30	G. Hastings (Scotland v Tonga, 1995)

Most tries by a player in a match:

6	M. Ellis (New Zealand v Japan, 1995)
4	I. Evans (Wales v Canada, 1987)
	J. Gallagher (New Zealand v Fiji, 1987)
	B. Robinson (Ireland v Zimbabwe, 1991)
	C. Green (New Zealand v Fiji, 1987)
	G. Hastings (Scotland v Ivory Coast, 1995)
	C. Williams (South Africa v Western Samoa, 1995)
	J. Lomu (New Zealand v England, 1995)

Most points in one tournament:

126	G. Fox (New Zealand, 1987)
112	T. Lacroix (France, 1995)
104	G. Hastings (Scotland, 1995)

Leading aggregate World Cup scorers:

227	G. Hastings (Scotland, 1987, 1991, 1995)
195	M. Lynagh (Australia, 1987, 1991, 1995)
170	G. Fox (New Zealand, 1987, 1991)

Most tries in World Cups:

11	R. Underwood (England, 1987, 1991, 1995)
10	D. Campese (Australia, 1987, 1991, 1995)
9	G. Hastings (Scotland, 1987, 1991, 1995)

Most tries in one tournament:

7	M. Ellis (New Zealand, 1995)
	J. Lomu (New Zealand, 1995)
6	D. Campese (Australia, 1991)
	C. Green (New Zealand, 1987)
	J. Kirwan (New Zealand, 1987)
	J-B. Lafond (France, 1991)

Most tries in a match by a team:

21	New Zealand v Japan (Bloemfontein, 1995)

Most penalty goals in World Cups:

31	M. Lynagh (Australia, 1987, 1991, 1995)
29	T. Lacroix (France, 1991, 1995)
27	G. Fox (New Zealand, 1987, 1991)

Most penalty goals in one tournament:

26	T. Lacroix (France, 1995)
21	G. Fox (New Zealand, 1987)
20	R. Andrew (England, 1995)

Most conversions in World Cups:

39	G. Hastings (Scotland, 1987, 1991, 1995)
37	G. Fox (New Zealand, 1987, 1991)
36	M. Lynagh (Australia, 1987, 1991, 1995)

Most conversions in one tournament:

30	G. Fox (New Zealand, 1987)
20	M. Lynagh (Australia, 1987)
	S. Culhane (New Zealand, 1995)

Most dropped goals in World Cups:

5	R. Andrew (England, 1987, 1991, 1995)
3	J. Davies (Wales, 1987)
	A. Mehrtens (New Zealand, 1995)
	J. Stransky (South Africa, 1995)

Most dropped goals in one tournament:

3	J. Davies (Wales, 1987)
	R. Andrew (England, 1995)
	A. Mehrtens (New Zealand, 1995)
	J. Stransky (South Africa, 1995)

Most dropped goals in one match by a team:

3	Fiji v Romania (Brive, 1991)

Leading try-scorers 1995:

Marc Ellis	New Zealand	7
Jonah Lomu	New Zealand	7
Gavin Hastings	Scotland	5
Rory Underwood	England	5
Thierry Lacroix	France	4
Adriaan Richter	South Africa	4
Chester Williams	South Africa	4
Philippe Saint-André	France	3
Gareth Thomas	Wales	3
Glen Osborne	New Zealand	3
Walter Little	New Zealand	3
Josh Kronfeld	New Zealand	3
Eric Rush	New Zealand	3
Jeffrey Wilson	New Zealand	3
Joe Roff	Australia	3
George Harder	Western Samoa	3
Paolo Vaccari	Italy	3

Most conversions 1995:

Simon Culhane	New Zealand	20
Gavin Hastings	Scotland	14
Andrew Mehrtens	New Zealand	14
Neil Jenkins	Wales	7
Thierry Lacroix	France	7
Paul Burke	Ireland	6
Eric Elwood	Ireland	5
Rob Andrew	England	5
Michael Lynagh	Australia	5
Diego Dominguez	Italy	5

Most penalty goals 1995:

Thierry Lacroix	France	26
Rob Andrew	England	20
Gavin Hastings	Scotland	17
Andrew Mehrtens	New Zealand	14
Joel Stransky	South Africa	13
Michael Lynagh	Australia	9
Neil Jenkins	Wales	8
Darren Kellett	Western Samoa	7
Diego Dominguez	Italy	7
Gareth Rees	Canada	6

Dropped-goals 1995:

Rob Andrew	England	3
Andrew Mehrtens	New Zealand	3
Joel Stransky	South Africa	3
Neil Jenkins	Wales	2
Yann Delaigue	France	1
Mike Catt	England	1
Ilie Ivanciuc	Romania	1
Zinzan Brooke	New Zealand	1
Gareth Rees	Canada	1
Diego Dominguez	Italy	1

Points scored (top 10) 1995

Thierry Lacroix	France	112
Gavin Hastings	Scotland	104
Andrew Mehrtens	New Zealand	84
Rob Andrew	England	79
Joel Stransky	South Africa	61
Michael Lynagh	Australia	47
Simon Culhane	New Zealand	45
Neil Jenkins	Wales	44
Diego Dominguez	Italy	39
Marc Ellis	New Zealand	35
Jonah Lomu	New Zealand	35

We've come a long way.

Funny country, South Africa.

Strange people.

Take our attitude to Chester Williams.

Generally speaking, he was regarded as a very good provinicial player. But good enough for the national side?

We weren't so sure. And if he was an affirmative action choice, we weren't comfortable.

The fact is, Chester was going to have to be better than the next man just to convince us he was as good.

And, bless him, he did it.

Once in the green and gold we saw that this little big man had verve, resilience, guts and something else. Instinctively, you warm to him.

Chester was important to this country as a sign to the outside world and, critically, to ourselves, of what was possible. He epitomised, "One team, one country".

But he was equally important as an inspirational player.

For these reasons we at SAA saw him as the perfect emblem of our promotion of the World Cup.

Grace under pressure is an exquisite test for measuring the individual. When Chester withdrew himself from the squad, the act merely confirmed the calibre of man we were losing.

It was a blow felt by a nation.

In some perverse way, it also fueled that part of tı South African psyche that makes us knock ourselves.

We aren't good enough to get past the quarter finals: o kickers are inconsistent, we don't win enough line-out ba our discipline is suspect.

In fact, to be perfectly honest, maybe we shouldn't ı staging the event.

Our hotels will be swamped, our airports won't be at to cope, the people in our service industries don't have clue what good service is. And so on.

Well, let's do a quick review.

As host country, by no means have we come close perfection. In many ways, we've been learning on the job.

And the aggression of our players, which seeminç gained an edge of meanness during the wilderness yeaı left us rueing an unfriendly evening in the Friendly City.

On the other hand, there's an awful lot of light on tı bright side.

Thursday 25th May was an etched-in-the-memory dɛ

The opening ceremony, with its simplicity, its precisiç its joyousness, its South Africanness, and its Nelson Mande

mpted tears of pride. We were world class.

This alone would have been sufficient to make our day.

the South African team elevated us to nirvana with a

ory few of us expected.

Despite the flood of returned tickets from abroad, the

ches attracted big crowds. Takings exceeded budget.

Overseas visitors at the games clearly enjoyed themselves.

hotels proved more than adequate. The airports, handling

adrons of small planes in addition to heavy commercial

edules, more than answered the call.

Well done to those in restaurants, hotels, pubs and shops

went out of their way to meet the needs of visitors.

to the taxi, bus and car hire people who ferried so many

cheerfully.

Well done to the crowds who gave good-natured support

all teams, and whose vociferous championing of the

erdogs helped minimise differences in skill levels.

Well done to the many ordinary South Africans who

ended tourists. And to the individuals and organisations

swathed a stricken young footballer in compassion.

Well done to those who took part in the opening and

ng ceremonies.

Well done to the 10 000 or so of our own SAA people – the cabin crews and pilots, the backroom heroes, and the airport staff around the world who gave meaning to our slogan, "Africa's warmest welcome".

And well done SARFU, 28 magnificent players, a canny coach and an exemplary manager.

Let's all take some credit, Rugby World Cup '95 has been a thundering success.

We aren't suggesting self-congratulation. Surely, though, we can shrug off the self-deprecation.

None of the predicted organisational disasters have occurred. Even those teams who left for home early took good memories with them. Coming through hell and high water, South Africa made the final.

And marvellously, appropriately, deservedly, Chester was there at the end.

POOL A

Newlands, Cape Town 25.05.95

Australia (13) 18 – 27 (14) South Africa

Tries: Lynagh, Kearns	*Tries:* Hendriks, Stransky
Cons: Lynagh	*Cons:* Stransky
Pens: Lynagh (2)	*Pens:* Stransky (4)
	DG: Stransky

Officials: Derek Bevan (Wal), Stephen Hilditch (Ire), C. Thomas (Wal).

Australia		**South Africa**	
	1 Dan Crowley		1 Pieter du Randt
15 Matthew Pini	2 Phil Kearns	15 André Joubert	2 James Dalton
14 Damian Smith	3 Ewen McKenzie	14 James Small	3 Balie Swart
13 Daniel Herbert	4 Rod McCall	13 Japie Mulder	4 Mark Andrews
12 Jason Little	5 John Eales	12 Hennie le Roux	5 Hannes Strydom
11 David Campese	6 Willie Ofahengaue	11 Pieter Hendriks	6 François Pienaar (c)
10 Michael Lynagh (c)	7 David Wilson	10 Joel Stransky	7 Ruben Kruger
9 George Gregan	8 Tim Gavin	9 Joost van der Westhuizen	8 Rudolf Straeuli
16 Matthew Burke	19 Troy Coker	16 Johan Roux	19 Chris Rossouw
17 Scott Bowen	20 Mark Hartill	17 Brendan Venter	20 Garry Pagel
18 Peter Slattery	21 Michael Foley	18 Gavin Johnson	21 Krynauw Otto

Boet Erasmus, Port Elizabeth 26.05.94

Canada (11) 34 – 3 (3) Romania

Tries: Snow, Charron, McKenzie	*Pens:* Nichitean
Cons: Rees (2)	
Pens: Rees (4)	
DG: Rees	

Officials: Colin Hawke (NZ), David Bishop (NZ), D.on Reordan (USA)

Canada		**Romania**	
	1 Eddie Evans		1 Gheorghe Leonte
15 Scott Stewart	2 Mark Cardinal	15 Gheorghe Solomie	2 Ionel Negreci
14 Winston Stanley	3 Rod Snow	14 Lucian Colceriu	3 Gabriel Vlad
13 Christian Stewart	4 Glen Ennis	13 Nicolae Raceanu	4 Sandu Ciorascu (c)
12 Steve Gray	5 Mike James	12 Romeo Gontineac	5 Constantin Cojocariu
11 David Lougheed	6 Al Charron	11 Ionel Rotaru	6 Traian Oroian
10 Gareth Rees (c)	7 Ian Gordon	10 Neculai Nichitean	7 Alexandru Gealapu
9 John Graf	8 Colin McKenzie	9 Daniel Neaga	8 Ovidiu Slusariuc
16 Ron Toews	19 John Hutchinson	16 Ilie Ivanciuc	19 Andrei Guranescu
17 Alan Tynan	20 Paul LeBlanc	17 Adrian Lungu	20 Leodor Costea
18 Gareth Rowlands	21 Karl Svoboda	18 Vasile Flutur	21 Valere Tufa

Newlands, Cape Town 30.05.95

South Africa (8) 21 – 8 (0) Romania

Tries: Richter (2)	*Tries:* Guranescu
Cons: Johnson	*Pens:* Ivanciuc
Pens: Johnson (3)	

Officials: Ken McCartney (Sco), Jim Fleming (Sco), Felise Vito (Sam)

South Africa		**Romania**	
	1 Garry Pagel		1 Gheorghe Leonte
15 Gavin Johnson	2 Chris Rossouw	15 Vasile Brici	2 Ionel Negreci
14 James Small	3 Marius Hurter	14 Lucian Colceriu	3 Gabriel Vlad
13 Christiaan Scholtz	4 Kobus Wiese	13 Nicolae Raceanu	4 Sandu Ciorascu
12 Brendan Venter	5 Krynauw Otto	12 Romeo Gontineac	5 Constantin Cojocariu
11 Pieter Hendriks	6 Ruben Kruger	11 Gheorghe Solomie	6 Andrei Guranescu
10 Hennie le Roux	7 Robby Brink	10 Ilie Ivanciuc	7 Alexandru Gealapu
9 Johan Roux	8 Adriaan Richter (c)	9 Vasile Flutur	8 Tiberiu Brinza (c)
16 André Joubert	19 Rudolf Straeuli	16 Neculai Nichitean	19 Ovidiu Slusariuc
17 Joel Stransky	20 Pieter du Randt	17 Adrian Lungu	20 Leodor Costea
18 Joost van der Westhuizen	21 James Dalton	18 Daniel Neaga	21 Valere Tufa

Boet Erasmus, Port Elizabeth 31.05.95

Australia (20) 27 – 11 (6) Canada

Tries: Tabua, Roff, Lynagh	*Tries:* Charron
Cons: Lynagh (3)	*Pens:* Rees (2)
Pens: Lynagh (2)	

Officials: Patrick Robin (Fra), Joel Dumé (F ra), Don Reordan (USA)

Australia		**Canada**	
	1 Tony Daly		1 Eddie Evans
15 Matthew Burke	2 Phil Kearns	15 Scott Stewart	2 Karl Svoboda
14 Joe Roff	3 Mark Hartill	14 Winston Stanley	3 Rod Snow
13 Jason Little	4 Warwick Waugh	13 Christian Stewart	4 Mike James
12 Tim Horan	5 John Eales	12 Steve Gray	5 Gareth Rowlands
11 David Campese	6 Willie Ofahengaue	11 David Lougheed	6 John Hutchinson
10 Michael Lynagh (c)	7 Ilie Tabua	10 Gareth Rees (c)	7 Gordon MacKinnon
9 Peter Slattery	8 Tim Gavin	9 John Graf	8 Al Charron
16 Matthew Pini	19 David Wilson	16 Ron Toews	19 Glen Ennis
17 Scott Bowen	20 Ewen McKenzie	17 Alan Tynan	20 Paul LeBlanc
18 George Gregan	21 Michael Foley	18 Ian Gordon	21 Mark Cardinal

Boet Erasmus Stadium, Port Elizabeth 03.06.95

Canada (0) 0 – 20 (17) South Africa

	Tries: Richter (2)
	Cons: Stransky (2)
	Pens: Stransky (2)

Officials: David McHugh (Ire), Stephen Hilditch (Ire), Steve Lander (Eng)

Canada		**South Africa**	
	1 Eddie Evans		1 Garry Pagel
15 Scott Stewart	2 Mark Cardinal	15 André Joubert	2 James Dalton
14 Winston Stanley	3 Rod Snow	14 Gavin Johnson	3 Marius Hurter
13 Christian Stewart	4 Al Charron	13 Christiaan Scholtz	4 Kobus Wiese
12 Steve Gray	5 Glen Ennis	12 Brendan Venter	5 Hannes Strydom
11 David Lougheed	6 Ian Gordon	11 Pieter Hendriks	6 François Pienaar (c)
10 Gareth Rees (c)	7 Gordon MacKinnon	10 Joel Stransky	7 Robby Brink
9 John Graf	8 Colin McKenzie	9 Johan Roux	8 Adriaan Richter
16 Ron Toews	19 Chris Michaluk	16 Ruben Kruger	19 Krynauw Otto
17 Alan Tynan	20 Paul LeBlanc	17 Hennie le Roux	20 Pieter du Randt
18 John Hutchinson	21 Karl Svoboda	18 Joost vd Westhuizen	21 Chris Rossouw

Danie Craven Stadium, Stellenbosch 03.06.95

Australia (14) 42 – 3 (3) Romania

Tries: Roff (2), Foley, Wilson, Burke, Smith	*DG:* Ivanciuc
Cons: Burke (2), Eales (4)	

Officials: Naoki Saito (Jap), David Bishop (NZ), Claudio Giacomel (Ita)

Australia		**Romania**	
	1 Tony Daly		1 Gheorghe Leonte
15 Matthew Burke	2 Michael Foley	15 Vasile Brici	2 Ionel Negreci
14 Damian Smith	3 Ewen McKenzie	14 Lucian Colceriu	3 Gabriel Vlad
13 Daniel Herbert	4 Rod McCall (c)	13 Nicolae Raceanu	4 Sandu Ciorascu
12 Tim Horan	5 John Eales	12 Romeo Gontineac	5 Constantin Cojocariu
11 Joe Roff	6 Ilie Tabua	11 Gheorghe Solomie	6 Andrei Guranescu
10 Scott Bowen	7 David Wilson	10 Ilie Ivanciuc	7 Alexandru Gealapu
9 George Gregan	8 Tim Gavin	9 Vasile Flutur	8 Tiberiu Brinza (c)
16 Matthew Pini	19 Daniel Manu	16 Ionel Rotaru	19 Traian Oroian
17 Michael Lynagh	20 Dan Crowley	17 Adrian Lungu	20 Leodor Costea
18 Peter Slattery	21 Phil Kearns	18 Daniel Neaga	21 Valere Tufa

POOL B

Kings Park, Durban 27.05.95

England (12) 24 – 18 (0) Argentina

Pens: Andrew (7)	*Tries:* Noriega, Arbizu
DG: Andrew	*Cons:* Arbizu
	Pens: Crexell, Arbizu

Officials: Jim Fleming (Sco), Ken McCartney (Sco), Moon Soo Han (Kor)

England		**Argentina**	
	1 Jason Leonard		1 Matias Corral
15 Mike Catt	2 Brian Moore	15 Ezequiel Jurado	2 Féderico Mendez
14 Tony Underwood	3 Victor Ubogu	14 Martin Teran	3 Patricio Noriega
13 Will Carling (c)	4 Martin Johnson	13 Diego Cuesta Silva	4 German Llanes
12 Jeremy Guscott	5 Martin Bayfield	12 Sebastian Salvat (c)	5 Pedro Sporleder
11 Rory Underwood	6 Tim Rodber	11 Diego Albanese	6 Rolando Martin
10 Rob Andrew	7 Ben Clarke	10 Lisandro Arbizu	7 Cristian Viel
9 Dewi Morris	8 Steve Ojomoh	9 Rodrigo Crexell	8 José Santamarina
16 Jonathan Callard	19 Neil Back	16 Ricardo le Fort	19 Agustin Pichot
17 Philip de Glanville	20 Graham Rowntree	17 Marcelo Urbano	20 G. del Castillo
18 Kyran Bracken	21 Graham Dawe	18 Sebastian Irazoqui	21 F. del Castillo

Basil Kenyon Stadium, East London 27.05.95

Western Samoa (12) 42 – 18 (11) Italy

Tries: Lima (2), Harder (2), Tatupu, Kellett	*Tries:* Ravazzolo, Vaccari
Cons: Kellett (3)	*Cons:* Dominguez
Pens: Kellett (2)	*Pens:* Dominguez
	DG: Dominguez

Officials: Joel Dumé (Fra), Patrick Robin (Fra), David McHugh (Ire)

Western Samoa		**Italy**	
	1 Michael Mika		1 Massimo Cuttitta (c)
15 Michael Umaga	2 Tala Leiasamaivao	15 Paolo Vaccari	2 Carlo Orlandi
14 Brian Lima	3 Peter Fatialofa (c)	14 Massimo Ravazzolo	3 Franco Properzi Curti
13 To'o Vaega	4 Lio Falaniko	13 Ivan Francescato	4 Paolo Pedroni
12 Tupo Fa'amasino	5 Daryl Williams	12 Massimo Bonomi	5 Roberto Favaro
11 George Harder	6 Sila Vaifale	11 Marcello Cuttitta	6 Orazio Arancio
10 Darren Kellett	7 Peter Junior Paramore	10 Diego Dominguez	7 Julian Gardner
9 Tuetu Nu'ualiitia	8 Shem Tatupu	9 Alessandro Troncon	8 Carlo Checchinato
16 George Leaupepe	19 Malaki Iupeli	16 Stefano Bordon	19 Andrea Sgorlon
17 Fata Sini	20 Potu Leavasa	17 Francesco Mazzariol	20 Andrea Castellani
18 Va'apu'u Vitale	21 George Latu	18 Luigi Troiani	21 Mauro Dal Sie

Basil Kenyon Stadium, East London 30.05.95

Western Samoa (10) 32 – 26 (16) Argentina

Tries: Harder, Leaupepe, Lam	*Tries:* pen try, Crexell
Cons: Kellett	*Cons:* Cilley (2)
Pens: Kellett (5)	*Pens:* Cilley (4)

Officials: David Bishop (NZ), Colin Hawke (NZ), Joel Dumé (Fra)

Western Samoa		**Argentina**	
	1 Michael Mika		1 Matias Corral
15 Michael Umaga	2 Tala Le'iasamaivao	15 Ezequiel Jurado	2 Féderico Mendez
14 Brian Lima	3 George Latu	14 Diego Cuesta Silva	3 Patricio Noriega
13 To'o Vaega	4 Potu Leavasa	13 Lisandro Arbizu	4 German Llanes
12 Tupo Fa'amasino	5 Lio Falaniko	12 Sebastian Salvat (c)	5 Pedro Sporleder
11 George Harder	6 Shem Tatupu	11 Martin Teran	6 Rolando Martin
10 Darren Kellett	7 Peter Junior Paramore	10 José Cilley	7 Cristian Viel
9 Tuetu Nu'uali'itia	8 Pat Lam (c)	9 Rodrigo Crexell	8 José Santamarina
16 George Leaupepe	19 Daryl Williams	16 Ricardo Le Fort	19 Agustin Pichot
17 Fata Sini	20 Brendan Reidy	17 Marcelo Urbano	20 F. del Castillo
8 Va'apu'u Vitale	21 Peter Fatialofa	18 Sebastian Irazoqui	21 Diego Albanese

King's Park, Durban 31.05.95

England (16) 27 – 20 (10) Italy

Tries: T Underwood, R Underwood	*Tries:* Vaccari, Cuttitta
Cons: Andrew	*Cons:* Dominguez (2)
Pens: Andrew (5)	*Pens:* Dominguez (2)

Officials: Stephen Hilditch (Ire), David McHugh (Ire), Niculae Chiciu (Rom)

England		**Italy**	
	1 Graham Rowntree		1 Massimo Cuttitta (c)
15 Mike Catt	2 Brian Moore	15 Luigi Troiani	2 Carlo Orlandi
14 Tony Underwood	3 Jason Leonard	14 Paolo Vaccari	3 Franco Properzi Curti
13 Philip de Glanville	4 Martin Johnson	13 Stefano Bordon	4 Pierpaolo Pedroni
12 Jeremy Guscott	5 Martin Bayfield	12 Ivan Francescato	5 Mark Giacheri
11 Rory Underwood	6 Tim Rodber	11 Mario Gerosa	6 Orazio Arancio
10 Rob Andrew (c)	7 Neil Back	10 Diego Dominguez	7 Andrea Sgorlon
9 Kyran Bracken	8 Ben Clarke	9 Alessandro Troncon	8 Julian Gardner
16 Jonathan Callard	19 Steve Ojomoh	16 Massimo Ravazzolo	19 Roberto Favaro
17 Damian Hopley	20 Graham Dawe	17 Francesco Mazzariol	20 Mauro Dal Sie
18 Dewi Morris	21 John Mallett	18 Massimo Capuzzoni	21 Moreno Trevisiol

King's Park, Durban 04.06.95

England (21) 44 – 22 (0) Western Samoa

Tries: Underwood (2), Back, Pen try	*Tries:* Sini (2), Umaga
Cons: Callard (3)	*Cons:* Fa'amasino (2)
Pens: Callard (5)	*Pens:* Fa'amasino
DG: Catt	

Officials: Patrick Robin (Fra), Joel Dumé (Fra), Jim Fleming (Sco)

England		**Western Samoa**	
	1 Graham Rowntree		1 Michael Mika
15 Jonathan Callard	2 Graham Dawe	15 Michael Umaga	2 Tala Leiasamaivo
14 Ian Hunter	3 Victor Ubogu	14 Brian Lima	3 George Latu
13 Will Carling (c)	4 Martin Johnson	13 To'o Vaega	4 Daryl Williams
12 Philip de Glanville	5 Richard West	12 Tupo Fa'amasino	5 Lio Falaniko
11 Rory Underwood	6 Steve Ojomoh	11 George Leaupepe	6 Potu Leavasa
10 Mike Catt	7 Neil Back	10 Esera Puleitu	7 Shem Tatupu
9 Dewi Morris	8 Dean Richards	9 Tuetu Nu'uali'itia	8 Pat Lam (c)
16 Damian Hopley	19 Tim Rodber	16 Fereti Tuilagi	19 Malaki Iupeli
17 Rob Andrew	20 Brian Moore	17 Fata Sini	20 Saini Lemanea
18 Kyran Bracken	21 John Mallett	18 Va'apu'u Vitale	21 Peter Fatialofa

Basil Kenyon Stadium, East London 04.06.95

Argentina (12) 25 – 31 (12) Italy

Tries: Martin,   Tries: Vaccari, Gerosa,
Corral, Cilley,   Dominguez
Pen try   Cons: Dominguez (2)
Cons: Cilley   Pens: Dominguez (4)
Pens: Cilley

Officials: Clayton Thomas (Wal), Derek Bevan (Wal), Koffi Seraphin (Iv)

Argentina		Italy	
15 Ezequiel Jurado	1 Matias Corral		1 Massimo Cuttitta (c)
14 Diego Cuesta Silva	2 Federico Mendez	15 Luigi Troiani	2 Carlo Orlandi
13 Lisandro Arbizu	3 Patricio Noriega	14 Paolo Vaccari	3 Franco Properzi Curti
12 Sebastian Salvat (c)	4 German Llanes	13 Stefano Bordon	4 Paolo Pedroni
11 Martin Teran	5 Pedro Sporleder	12 Ivan Francescato	5 Mark Giacheri
10 José Cilley	6 Rolando Martin	11 Mario Gerosa	6 Orazio Arancio
9 Rodrigo Crexell	7 Cristian Viel	10 Diego Dominguez	7 Andrea Sgorlon
	8 Jose Santamarina	9 Alessandro Troncon	8 Julian Gardner
16 Ricardo le Fort	19 Agustin Pichot	16 Massimo Ravazzolo	19 Roberto Favaro
17 Marcelo Urbano	20 F. del Castillo	17 Francesco Mazzariol	20 Mauro Dal Sie
18 Sebastian Irazoqui	21 G. del Castillo	18 Massimo Capuzzoni	21 Moreno Trevisiol

POOL C

Free State Stadium, Bloemfontein 27.05.95

Wales (36) 57 – 10 (0) Japan

Tries: Thomas (3),   Tries: Oto (2)
Evans (2), Moore, Taylor
Cons: Jenkins (5)
Pens: Jenkins (4)

Officials: Efraim Sklar (Arg), Stephen Hilditch (Ire), Claudio Giacomel (Ita)

Wales		Japan	
15 Anthony Clement	1 Mike Griffiths		1 Osamu Ota
14 Ieuan Evans	2 Garin Jenkins	15 Tsutomu Matsuda	2 Masahiro Kunda (c)
13 Mike Hall (c)	3 John Davies	14 Lopeti-Tuimo Oto	3 Kazuaki Takahashi
12 Neil Jenkins	4 Derwyn Jones	13 Akira Yoshida	4 Yoshihiko Sakuraba
11 Gareth Thomas	5 Gareth Llewellyn	12 Yukio Motoki	5 Bruce Ferguson
10 Adrian Davies	6 Stuart Davies	11 Terunori Masuho	6 Hiroyuki Kajihara
9 Andrew Moore	7 Hemi Taylor	10 Seiji Hirao	7 Sinali Latu
	8 Emyr Lewis	9 Masami Horikoshi	8 Sione Latu
16 Wayne Proctor	19 Stuart Roy	16 Wataru Murata	19 Eiji Hirotsu
17 David Evans	20 Ricky Evans	17 Katsuhiro Matsuo	20 Masanori Takura
18 Robert Jones	21 Jonathan Humphreys	18 Kiyoshi Imaizumi	21 Ko Izawa

Ellis Park, Johannesburg 27.05.95

New Zealand (20) 43 – 19 (12) Ireland

Tries: Lomu (2),   Tries: Halpin,
Bunce, Osborne,   McBride, Corkery
Kronfeld   Cons: Elwood (2)
Cons: Mehrtens (3)
Pens: Mehrtens (4)

Officials: Wayne Erickson (Aus), Barry Leask (Aus), George Gadjovich (Can)

New Zealand		Ireland	
15 Glen Osborne	1 Craig Dowd		1 Nick Popplewell
14 Jeff Wilson	2 Sean Fitzpatrick (c)	15 Jim Staples	2 Terry Kingston (c)
13 Frank Bunce	3 Olo Brown	14 Richard Wallace	3 Garrett Halpin
12 Walter Little	4 Ian Jones	13 Brendan Mullin	4 Gabriel Fulcher
11 Jonah Lomu	5 Blair Larsen	12 Jonathan Bell	5 Neil Francis
10 Andrew Mehrtens	6 Jamie Joseph	11 Simon Geoghegan	6 David Corkery
9 Graeme Bachop	7 Josh Kronfeld	10 Eric Elwood	7 Denis McBride
	8 Mike Brewer	9 Michael Bradley	8 Paddy Johns
16 Marc Ellis	19 Kevin Schuler	16 Maurice Field	19 Anthony Foley
17 Simon Culhane	20 Richard Loe	17 Paul Burke	20 Paul Wallace
18 Ant Strachan	21 Norm Hewitt	18 Niall Hogan	21 Keith Wood

Free State Stadium, Bloemfontein 31.05.95

Ireland (19) 50 – 28 (14) Japan

Tries: Pen try (2),   Tries: Sinali Latu,
Corkery, Francis, Izawa, Hirao, Takura
Geoghegan, Halvey, Cons: Yoshida (4)
Hogan
Cons: Burke (6)
Pens: Burke

Officials: Stef Neethling (RSA), Ian Rogers (RSA), Etoni Tonga (Ton)

Ireland		Japan	
15 Conor O'Shea	1 Nick Popplewell (c)		1 Osamu Ota
14 Richard Wallace	2 Keith Wood	15 Tsutomu Matsuda	2 Masahiro Kunda (c)
13 Brendan Mullin	3 Paul Wallace	14 Lopeti-Tuimo Oto	3 Masanori Takura
12 Maurice Field	4 David Tweed	13 Akira Yoshida	4 Yoshihiko Sakuraba
11 Simon Geoghegan	5 Neil Francis	12 Yukio Motoki	5 Bruce Ferguson
10 Paul Burke	6 David Corkery	11 Yoshihito Yoshida	6 Hiroyuki Kajihara
9 Niall Hogan	7 Eddie Halvey	10 Seiji Hirao	7 Sinali Latu
	8 Paddy Johns	9 Masami Horikoshi	8 Sione Latu
16 Philip Danaher	19 Anthony Foley	16 Wataru Murata	19 Eiji Hirotsu
17 Eric Elwood	20 Garrett Halpin	17 Yoshiji Hirose	20 Kazuaki Takahashi
18 Michael Bradley	21 Terry Kingston	18 Kiyoshi Imaizumi	21 Ko Izawa

Ellis Park, Johannesburg 31.05.95

New Zealand (20) 34 – 9 (6) Wales

Tries: Little, Ellis, Kronfeld Pens: Jenkins (2)
Cons: Mehrtens (2)   DG: Jenkins
Pens: Mehrtens (4)
DG: Mehrtens

Officials: Ed Morrison (Eng), Steve Lander (Eng), Barry Leask (Aus)

New Zealand		Wales	
15 Glen Osborne	1 Craig Dowd		1 Ricky Evans
14 Marc Ellis	2 Sean Fitzpatrick (c)	15 Anthony Clement	2 Jonathan Humphreys
13 Frank Bunce	3 Olo Brown	14 Ieuan Evans	3 John Davies
12 Walter Little	4 Ian Jones	13 Mike Hall (c)	4 Derwyn Jones
11 Jonah Lomu	5 Blair Larsen	12 Gareth Thomas	5 Greg Prosser
10 Andrew Mehrtens	6 Jamie Joseph	11 Wayne Proctor	6 Gareth Llewellyn
9 Graeme Bachop	7 Josh Kronfeld	10 Neil Jenkins	7 Mark Bennett
	8 Mike Brewer	9 Robert Jones	8 Hemi Taylor
16 Eric Rush	19 Kevin Schuler	16 Steve Ford	19 Emyr Lewis
17 Simon Culhane	20 Richard Loe	17 David Evans	20 Mike Griffiths
18 Ant Strachan	21 Norm Hewitt	18 Andrew Moore	21 Garin Jenkins

Free State Stadium, Bloemfontein 04.06.95

New Zealand (84) 145 – 17 (3) Japan

Tries: Ellis (6),   Tries: Kajihara (2)
Rush (3), Wilson (3), Cons: Hirose (2)
Osborne (2),   Pens: Hirose
Brooke (2),
Ieremia, Culhane, Loe
Dowd, Henderson
Cons: Culhane (20)

Officials: George Gadjovich (Can), Ed Morrison (Eng), Niculae Chiciu (Rom)

New Zealand		Japan	
15 Glen Osborne	1 Craig Dowd		1 Osamu Ota
14 Jeff Wilson	2 Norm Hewitt	15 Tsutomu Matsuda	2 Masahiro Kunda (c)
13 Marc Ellis	3 Richard Loe	14 Lopeti-Tuimo Oto	3 Kazuaki Takahashi
12 Alama Ieremia	4 Robin Brooke	13 Akira Yoshida	4 Yoshihiko Sakuraba
11 Eric Rush	5 Blair Larsen	12 Yukio Motoki	5 Bruce Ferguson
10 Simon Culhane	6 Kevin Schuler	11 Yoshihito Yoshida	6 Hiroyuki Kajihara
9 Ant Strachan	7 Paul Henderson	10 Keiji Hirose	7 Ko Izawa
	8 Zinzan Brooke	9 Wataru Murata	8 Sinali Latu
16 Walter Little	19 Jamie Joseph	16 Masami Horikoshi	19 Eiji Hirotsu
17 Andrew Mehrtens	20 Olo Brown	17 Katsuhiro Matsuo	20 Kazu Hamabe
18 Graeme Bachop	21 Sean Fitzpatrick	18 Kiyoshi Imaizumi	21 Takashi Akatsuka

Ellis Park, Johannesburg 04.06.95

Ireland (14) 24 – 23 (6) Wales

Tries: Popplewell,   Tries: Humphreys,
McBride, Halvey   Taylor
Cons: Elwood (3)   Cons: Jenkins (2)
Pens: Elwood   Pens: Jenkins (3)
DG: Davies

Officials: Ian Rogers (RSA), Stef Neethling (RSA), Moon Soo Han (Kor)

Ireland		Wales	
15 Conor O'Shea	1 Nick Popplewell		1 Mike Griffiths
14 Richard Wallace	2 Terry Kingston (c)	15 Anthony Clement	2 Jonathan Humphreys
13 Brendan Mullin	3 Gary Halpin	14 Ieuan Evans	3 John Davies
12 Jonathan Bell	4 Gabriel Fulcher	13 Mike Hall (c)	4 Derwyn Jones
11 Simon Geoghegan	5 Neil Francis	12 Neil Jenkins	5 Gareth Llewellyn
10 Eric Elwood	6 David Corkery	11 Gareth Thomas	6 Stuart Davies
9 Niall Hogan	7 Denis McBride	10 Adrian Davies	7 Hemi Taylor
	8 Paddy Johns	9 Robert Jones	8 Emyr Lewis
16 Philip Danaher	19 Eddie Halvey	16 Wayne Proctor	19 Greg Prosser
17 Paul Burke	20 Paul Wallace	17 David Evans	20 Ricky Evans
18 Michael Bradley	21 Shane Byrne	18 Andrew Moore	21 Garin Jenkins

POOL D

Olympia Park, Rustenburg 26.05.95

Scotland (34) 89 – 0 (0) Ivory Coast

Tries: Hastings (4),
Walton (2), Logan (2),
Chalmers, Stanger,
Burnell, Wright, Joiner
Cons: Hastings (9)
Pens: Hastings (2)

Officials: Felise Vito (Sam), Ian Rogers (RSA), Etoni Tonga (Ton)

Scotland		Ivory Coast	
15 Gavin Hastings (c)	1 Paul Burnell		1 Ernest Bley
14 Craig Joiner	2 Kevin McKenzie	15 Victor Kouassi	2 Edouard Angoran
13 Anthony Stanger	3 Peter Wright	14 Paulin Bouazo	3 Toussaint Djehi
12 Graham Shiel	4 Doddie Weir	13 Jean Sathicq	4 Gilbert Bado
11 Kenny Logan	5 Stewart Campbell	12 Lucien Niakou	5 Amidou Kone
10 Craig Chalmers	6 Peter Walton	11 Celestin N'Gbala	6 Patrice Pere
9 Bryan Redpath	7 Ian Smith	10 Athanase Dali	7 Ismaila Lassissi
	8 Rob Wainwright	9 Frederic Dupont	8 Djakaria Sanoko
16 Scott Hastings	19 Damian Cronin	16 Max Brito	19 Alfred Okou
17 Ian Jardine	20 John Manson	17 Aboubacar Camara	20 Jean-Pascal Ezoua
18 Derrick Patterson	21 Kenny Milne	18 Felix Dago	21 Achille Niamien

Loftus Versfeld, Pretoria 26.05.95

France (6) 38 – 10 (0) Tonga

Tries: Lacroix (2),   Tries: Va'enuku
Heuber, Saint-André Cons: Tu'ipulotu
Cons: Lacroix (3)   Pens: Tu'ipulotu
Pens: Lacroix (3)
DG: Delaigue

Officials: Steve Lander (Eng), E.d Morrison (Eng), Naoki Saito (Jap)

France		Tonga	
15 Jean-Luc Sadourny	1 Louis Armary		1 Sa'ili Fe'ao
14 Emile Ntamack	2 Jean-Michel Gonzalez	15 Sateki Tu'ipulotu	2 Fololisi Masila
13 Philippe Sella	3 Philippe Gallart	14 Alaska Taufa	3 Tu'akalau Fukofuka
12 Thierry Lacroix	4 Olivier Merle	13 Unuoi Va'enuku	4 William Lose
11 Philippe Saint-André	5 Olivier Brouzet	12 Penieli Latu	5 Falamani Mafi
10 Yann Delaigue	6 Philippe Benetton	11 Tevita Va'enuku	6 Felti Mahoni
9 Aubin Hueber	7 Marc Cecillon	10 'Elisi Vunipola	7 'polito Fenukitau
	8 Abdelatif Benazzi	9 Manu Vunipola	8 Manakaetau 'Otai (c)
16 Sebastien Viars	19 Laurent Cabannes	16 Taipe 'Isitolo	19 'Inoke Afeaki
17 Franck Mesnel	20 Marc de Rougement	17 'Akuila Mafi	20 'Etuini Talakai
18 Guy Accoceberry	21 Christian Califano	18 Nafe Tufui	21 Fe'ao Vunipola

Olympia Park, Rustenburg 30.05.94

France (28) 54 – 18 (3) Ivory Coast

Tries: Lacroix (2),   Tries: Camara, Soulama
Benazzi,   Cons: Kouassi
Accoceberry,   Pens: Kouassi (2)
Viars, Techoueyres,
Costes, Saint-André
Cons: Lacroix (2),
Deylaud (2)
Pens: Lacroix (2)

Officials: H Moon Soo (Kor), Derek Bevan (Wal), George Gadjovich (Can)

France		Ivory Coast	
15 Sebastien Viars	1 Laurent Benezech		1 Jean-Pascal Ezoua
14 William Techoueyres	2 Marc de Rougement	15 Victor Kouassi	2 Achille Niamien
13 Franck Mesnel	3 Christian Califano	14 Aboubacar Soulama	3 Toussaint Djehi
12 Thierry Lacroix	4 Olivier Brouzet	13 Jean Sathicq (c)	4 Ble Aka
11 Philippe Saint-André	5 Olivier Roumat	12 Lucien Niakou	5 Djakaria Sanoko
10 Yann Delaigue	6 Arnaud Costes	11 Max Brito	6 Patrice Pere
9 Guy Accoceberry	7 Laurent Cabannes	10 Aboubacar Camara	7 Alfred Okou
	8 Abdelatif Benazzi	9 Frederic Dupont	8 Ismaila Lassissi
16 Emile Ntamack	19 Philippe Benetton	16 Paulin Bouazo	19 Amidou Kone
17 Christophe Deylaud	20 Philippe Gallart	17 Thierry Kouame	20 Ernest Bley
18 Aubin Hueber	21 Jean-Michel Gonzalez	18 Felix Dago	21 Edouard Angoran

Loftus Versfeld, Pretoria 30.05.95

Scotland (18) 41 – 5 (5) Tonga

Tries: Peters, G Hastings, S Hastings — *Tries*: Fenukitau
Cons: G Hastings
Pens: G Hastings (8)

Officials: Barry Leask (Aus), Wayne Erickson (Aus), Naoki Saito (Jap)

Scotland		Tonga	
	1 David Hilton		1 Sa'ili Fe'ao
15 Gavin Hastings (c)	2 Kenny Milne	15 Sateki Tu'ipulotu	2 Fe'ao Vunipola
14 Craig Joiner	3 Peter Wright	14 Alaska Taufa	3 Tu'akalau Fukofuka
13 Scott Hastings	4 Damian Cronin	13 Unuoi Va'enuku	4 William Lose
12 Ian Jardine	5 Doddie Weir	12 Penieli Latu	5 Pouvalu Latukefu
11 Kenny Logan	6 Rob Wainwright	11 Tevita Va'enuku	6 'Inoke Afeaki
10 Craig Chalmers	7 Iain Morrison	10 'Elisi Vunipola	7 'Ipolito Fenukitau
9 Derrick Patterson	8 Eric Peters	9 Manu Vunipola	8 Manakaetau 'Otai (c)
16 Cameron Glasgow	19 Jeremy Richardson	16 Taipe 'Isitolo	19 Feleti Fakaongo
17 Graham Shiel	20 Paul Burnell	17 'Akuila Mafi	20 Alaska Taufa
18 Bryan Redpath	21 Kevin McKenzie	18 Nafe Tufui	21 Takau Lutua

Olympia Park, Rustenburg 03.06.95

Tonga (24) 29 – 11 (0) Ivory Coast

Tries: Latukefu, Otai, Tu' ipulotu, pen try — *Tries*: Okou
Cons: Tu' ipulotu (3) — *Pens*: Dali (2)
Pens: Tu' ipulotu

Officials: Don Reordan (USA), Ken McCartney (Sco), Efraim Sklar (Arg)

Tonga		Ivory Coast	
	1 Tu'akalau Fukofuka		1 Ernest Bley
15 Sateki Tu'ipulotu	2 Fe'ao Vunipola	15 Victor Kouassi	2 Edouard Angoran
14 Penieli Latu	3 'Etuini Talakai	14 Aboubacar Soulama	3 Toussaint Djehi
13 Simana Mafile'o	4 Pouvalu Latukefu	13 Jean Sathicq (c)	4 Gilbert Bado
12 Unuoi Va'enuku	5 'Akuila Mafi	12 Lucien Niakou	5 Amidou Kone
11 Tevita Va'enuku	6 'Inoke Afeaki	11 Max Brito	6 Patrice Pere
10 'Elisi Vunipola	7 William Lose	10 Aboubacar Camara	7 Alfred Okou
9 Nafe Tufui	8 Manakaetau 'Otai (c)	9 Frederic Dupont	8 Ismaila Lassissi
16 Taipe 'Isitolo	19 Feleti Fakaongo	16 Thierry Kouame	19 Djakaria Sanoko
17 Alaska Taufa	20 Takau Lutua	17 Athanase Dali	20 Daniel Quansah
18 'Akuila Mafi	21 Sa'ili Fe'ao	18 Felix Dago	21 Jean-Pascal Ezoua

Loftus Versfeld, Pretoria 03.06.95

Scotland (13) 19 – 22 (3) France

Try: Wainwright — *Try*: Ntamack
Cons: Hastings G — *Con*: Lacroix
Pens: Hastings G (4) — *Pens*: Lacroix (5)

Officials: Wayne Erickson (Aus), Barry Leask (Aus), Stef Neethling (RSA)

Scotland		France	
	1 David Hilton		1 Laurent Benezech
15 Gavin Hastings (c)	2 Kenny Milne	15 Jean-Luc Sadourny	2 Jean-Michel Gonzalez
14 Craig Joiner	3 Peter Wright	14 Emile Ntamack	3 Christian Califano
13 Scott Hastings	4 Damian Cronin	13 Philippe Sella	4 Olivier Merle
12 Graham Shiel	5 Doddie Weir	12 Thierry Lacroix	5 Olivier Roumat
11 Kenny Logan	6 Rob Wainwright	11 Philippe Saint-André	6 Abdelatif Benazzi
10 Craig Chalmers	7 Iain Morrison	10 Christophe Deylaud	7 Laurent Cabannes
9 Bryan Redpath	8 Eric Peters	9 Guy Accoceberry	8 Philippe Benetton
16 Tony Stanger	19 Stewart Campbell	16 Franck Mesnel	19 Marc Cecillon
17 Ian Jardine	20 Paul Burnell	17 Yann Delaigue	20 Philippe Gallart
18 Derrick Patterson	21 Kevin McKenzie	18 Aubin Hueber	21 Louis Armary

QUARTER-FINALS

King's Park, Durban 10.06.95

France (12) 36 – 12 (12) Ireland

Tries: Saint-André, Ntamack — *Pens*: Elwood (4)
Cons: Lacroix
Pens: Lacroix (8)

Officials: Ed Morrison (Eng),, Ian Rogers (SA), Steve Lander (Eng)

France		Ireland	
	1 Louis Armary		1 Nick Popplewell
15 Jean-Luc Sadourny	2 Jean-Michel Gonzalez	15 Conor O'Shea	2 Terry Kingston (c)
14 Emile Ntamack	3 Christian Califano	14 Darragh O'Mahony	3 Garrett Halpin
13 Philippe Sella	4 Olivier Merle	13 Brendan Mullin	4 Gabriel Fulcher
12 Thierry Lacroix	5 Olivier Roumat	12 Jonathan Bell	5 Neil Francis
11 Philippe Saint-André	6 Abdelatif Benazzi	11 Simon Geoghegan	6 David Corkery
10 Christophe Deylaud	7 Laurent Cabannes	10 Eric Elwood	7 Denis McBride
9 Aubin Hueber	8 Marc Cecillon	9 Niall Hogan	8 Paddy Johns
16 Franck Mesnel	19 Albert Cigagna	16 Philip Danaher	19 Eddie Halvey
17 Yann Delaigue	20 Philippe Gallart	17 Paul Burke	20 Paul Wallace
18 Fabien Galthié	21 Laurent Benezech	18 Michael Bradley	21 Shane Byrne

Ellis Park, Johannesburg 10.06.95

South Africa (23) 42 – 14 (0) Western Samoa

Tries: Williams (4), Rossouw, Andrews — *Tries*: Nu'uali'itia, Tatupu
Cons: Johnson (3) — *Cons*: Fa'amasino (2)
Pens: Johnson (2)

Officials: Jim Fleming (Sco), Patrick Robin (Fra), Joel Dumé(Fra)

South Africa		Western Samoa	
	1 Pieter du Randt		1 Michael Mika
15 André Joubert	2 Chris Rossouw	15 Michael Umaga	2 Tala Leiasamaivao
14 Gavin Johnson	3 Balie Swart	14 Brian Lima	3 George Latu
13 Christiaan Scholtz	4 Kobus Wiese	13 To'o Vaega	4 Saini Lemanea
12 Japie Mulder	5 Mark Andrews	12 Tupo Fa'amasino	5 Lio Falaniko
11 Chester Williams	6 François Pienaar (c)	11 George Harder	6 Shem Tatupu
10 Hennie le Roux	7 Ruben Kruger	10 Fata Sini	7 Peter Junior Paramore
9 Joost van der Westhuizen	8 Rudolf Straeuli	9 Tuetu Nu'uali'itia	8 Pat Lam (c)
16 Brendan Venter	19 Krynauw Otto	16 Fereti Tuilagi	19 Sam Kaleta
17 Johan Roux	20 Garry Pagel	17 Va'apu'u Vitale	20 Brendan Reidy
18 Adriaan Richter	21 Naka Drotské	18 Sila Vaifale	21 Peter Fatialofa

Newlands, Cape Town 11.06.95

England (13) 25 – 22 (6) Australia

Tries: T Underwood — *Tries*: Smith
Cons: Andrew — *Cons*: Lynagh
Pens: Andrew (5) — *Pens*: Lynagh (5)
DG: Andrew

Officials: David Bishop (NZ), Colin Hawke (NZ), Stephen Hilditch (Ire)

England		Australia	
	1 Jason Leonard		1 Dan Crowley
15 Mike Catt	2 Brian Moore	15 Matthew Burke	2 Phil Kearns
14 Tony Underwood	3 Victor Ubogu	14 Damian Smith	3 Ewen McKenzie
13 Will Carling (c)	4 Martin Johnson	13 Jason Little	4 Rod McCall
12 Jeremy Guscott	5 Martin Bayfield	12 Tim Horan	5 John Eales
11 Rory Underwood	6 Tim Rodber	11 David Campese	6 Willie Ofahengaue
10 Rob Andrew	7 Ben Clarke	10 Michael Lynagh (c)	7 David Wilson
9 Dewi Morris	8 Dean Richards	9 George Gregan	8 Tim Gavin
16 Jonathan Callard	19 Steve Ojomoh	16 Joe Roff	19 Daniel Manu
17 Philip de Glanville	20 Graham Dawe	17 Scott Bowen	20 Mark Hartill
18 Kyran Bracken	21 Graham Rowntree	18 Peter Slattery	21 Michael Foley

Loftus Versfeld, Pretoria 11.06.95

New Zealand (17) 48 – 30 (9) Scotland

Tries: Little (2), Bunce, Lomu, Mehrtens, Fitzpatrick — *Tries*: Weir (2), S Hastings
Cons: Mehrtens (6) — *Cons*: G Hastings (3)
Pens: Mehrtens (2) — *Pens*: G Hastings (3)

Officials: Derek Bevan (Wal), Wayne Erickson (Aus), Clayton Thomas (Wal)

New Zealand		Scotland	
	1 Richard Loe		1 David Hilton
15 Jeff Wilson	2 Sean Fitzpatrick (c)	15 Gavin Hastings (c)	2 Kenny Milne
14 Marc Ellis	3 Olo Brown	14 Craig Joiner	3 Peter Wright
13 Frank Bunce	4 Ian Jones	13 Scott Hastings	4 Damian Cronin
12 Walter Little	5 Robin Brooke	12 Graham Shiel	5 Doddie Weir
11 Jonah Lomu	6 Jamie Joseph	11 Kenny Logan	6 Rob Wainwright
10 Andrew Mehrtens	7 Josh Kronfeld	10 Craig Chalmers	7 Iain Morrison
9 Graeme Bachop	8 Zinzan Brooke	9 Bryan Redpath	8 Eric Peters
16 Alama Ieremia	19 Mike Brewer	16 Tony Stanger	19 Stewart Campbell
17 Simon Culhane	20 Craig Dowd	17 Ian Jardine	20 Paul Burnell
18 Ant Strachan	21 Norm Hewitt	18 Derrick Patterson	21 Kevin McKenzie

SEMI-FINALS

King's Park, Durban 17.06.95

France (6) 15 – 19 (10) South Africa

Pens: Lacroix (5) — *Tries*: Kruger
Cons: Stransky
Pens: Stransky (4)

Officials: Derek Bevan (Wal), Wayne Erickson (Aus), Clayton Thomas (Wal)

France		South Africa	
	1 Louis Armary		1 Pieter du Randt
15 Jean-Luc Sadourny	2 Jean-Michel Gonzalez	15 André Joubert	2 Chris Rossouw
14 Emile Ntamack	3 Christian Califano	14 James Small	3 Balie Swart
13 Philippe Sella	4 Olivier Merle	13 Japie Mulder	4 Kobus Wiese
12 Thierry Lacroix	5 Olivier Roumat	12 Hennie le Roux	5 Hannes Strydom
11 Philippe Saint-André	6 Abdelatif Benazzi	11 Chester Williams	6 François Pienaar (c)
10 Christophe Deylaud	7 Laurent Cabannes	10 Joel Stransky	7 Ruben Kruger
9 Fabien Galthié	8 Marc Cecillon	9 Joost van der Westhuizen	8 Mark Andrews
16 Franck Mesnel	19 Albert Cigagna	16 Gavin Johnson	19 Rudolf Straeuli
17 Yann Delaigue	20 Philippe Gallart	17 Christiaan Scholtz	20 Garry Pagel
18 Aubin Hueber	21 Laurent Benezech	18 Johan Roux	21 Naka Drotské

Newlands, Cape Town 18.06.95

New Zealand (25) 45 – 29 (3) England

Tries: Lomu (4), Bachop, Kronfeld — *Tries*: Carling (2), R Underwood (2)
Cons: Mehrtens (3) — *Cons*: Andrew (3)
Pens: Mehrtens — *Pens*: Andrew
DG: Z Brooke, Mehrtens.

Officials: Stephen Hilditch (Ire), Joel Dumé (Fra), Stef Neethling (RSA)

New Zealand		England	
	1 Craig Dowd		1 Jason Leonard
15 Glen Osborne	2 Sean Fitzpatrick (c)	15 Mike Catt	2 Brian Moore
14 Jeff Wilson	3 Olo Brown	14 Tony Underwood	3 Victor Ubogu
13 Frank Bunce	4 Ian Jones	13 Will Carling (c)	4 Martin Johnson
12 Walter Little	5 Robin Brooke	12 Jeremy Guscott	5 Martin Bayfield
11 Jonah Lomu	6 Mike Brewer	11 Rory Underwood	6 Tim Rodber
10 Andrew Mehrten	7 Josh Kronfeld	10 Rob Andrew	7 Ben Clarke
9 Graeme Bachop	8 Zinzan Brooke	9 Dewi Morris	8 Dean Richards
16 Marc Ellis	19 Blair Larsen	16 Jonathan Callard	19 Steve Ojomoh
17 Simon Culhane	20 Richard Loe	17 Philip de Glanville	20 Graham Dawe
18 Ant Strachan	21 Norm Hewitt	18 Kyran Bracken	21 Graham Rowntree

THIRD-PLACE PLAY-OFF

Loftus Versfeld, Pretoria 22.06.95

France (3) 19 – 9 (3) England

Tries: Roumat, Ntamack — *Pens*: Andrew (3)
Pens: Lacroix (3)

Officials: David Bishop (NZ), Colin Hawke (NZ), Wayne Erickson (Aus)

France		England	
	1 Laurent Benezech		1 Jason Leonard
15 Emile Ntamack	2 Jean-Michel Gonzalez	15 Mike Catt	2 Brian Moore
14 Jean-Luc Sadourny	3 Christian Califano	14 Ian Hunter	3 Victor Ubogu
13 Philippe Sella	4 Olivier Merle	13 Will Carling (c)	4 Martin Johnson
12 Thierry Lacroix	5 Olivier Roumat	12 Jeremy Guscott	5 Martin Bayfield
11 Philippe Saint-André	6 Abdelatif Benazzi	11 Rory Underwood	6 Tim Rodber
10 Franck Mesnel	7 Laurent Cabannes	10 Rob Andrew	7 Ben Clarke
9 Fabien Galthié	8 Albert Cigagna	9 Dewi Morris	8 Steve Ojomoh
16 Yann Delaigue	19 Olivier Brouzet	16 Jonathan Callard	19 Neil Back
17 Christophe Deylaud	20 Philippe Gallart	17 Philip de Glanville	20 Graham Dawe
18 Aubin Hueber	21 Marc de Rougemont	18 Kyran Bracken	21 Graham Rowntree

THE FINAL

Ellis Park, Johannesburg 24.06.95

South Africa (9) 15 – 12 (6) New Zealand

Pens: Stransky (3) — *Pens*: Mehrtens (3)
DG: Stransky (2) — *DG*: Mehrtens

Officials: Derek Bevan (Wal), Ed Morrison (Eng), Patrick Robin (Fra)

South Africa		New Zealand	
	1 Pieter du Randt		1 Craig Dowd
15 André Joubert	2 Chris Rossouw	15 Glen Osborne	2 Sean Fitzpatrick (c)
14 James Small	3 Balie Swart	14 Jeff Wilson	3 Olo Brown
13 Japie Mulder	4 Kobus Wiese	13 Frank Bunce	4 Ian Jones
12 Hennie le Roux	5 Hannes Strydom	12 Walter Little	5 Robin Brooke
11 Chester Williams	6 François Pienaar (c)	11 Jonah Lomu	6 Mike Brewer
10 Joel Stransky	7 Ruben Kruger	10 Andrew Mehrtens	7 Josh Kronfeld
9 Joost van der Westhuizen	8 Mark Andrews	9 Graeme Bachop	8 Zinzan Brooke
16 Gavin Johnson	19 Rudolf Straeuli	16 Marc Ellis	19 Jamie Joseph
17 Brendan Venter	20 Garry Pagel	17 Simon Culhane	20 Richard Loe
18 Johan Roux	21 Naka Drotské	18 Ant Strachan	21 Norm Hewitt

Famouse Grouse Rugby World Cup Awards:

Finest Performance by an Unseeded Team:	Italy
Finest Try:	Josh Kronfeld (NZ) – second try in the quarter-final against England.
Finest Moment:	Jonah Lomu (NZ)